Ordeal by Slander

By Owen Lattimore

The Desert Road to Turkestan

High Tartary

Manchuria, Cradle of Conflict

The Mongols of Manchuria

Inner Asian Frontiers of China

Mongol Journeys

America and Asia

China, a Short History
(*with Eleanor Lattimore*)

Solution in Asia

The Situation in Asia

Pivot of Asia

Ordeal by Slander

OWEN LATTIMORE

Ordeal by Slander

An Atlantic Monthly Press Book

Little, Brown and Company · Boston

1950

FIRST EDITION

Published July 1950

ATLANTIC–LITTLE, BROWN BOOKS
ARE PUBLISHED BY
LITTLE, BROWN AND COMPANY
IN ASSOCIATION WITH
THE ATLANTIC MONTHLY PRESS

*Published simultaneously
in Canada by McClelland and Stewart Limited*

PRINTED IN THE UNITED STATES OF AMERICA
BY THE HADDON CRAFTSMEN, INC., SCRANTON, PA.

FOREWORD

THIS BOOK is an account of what happened to me and my family when I was suddenly accused, without warrant or warning, of being "the top Russian espionage agent in this country." It is not written in self-defense. I made my defense, at length, before the Senate Subcommittee appointed to investigate charges of Communism in the Department of State.

In fitting together the narrative of what happened and the statements that I made before the Committee, the statements have been given in the form of condensed excerpts, in order to avoid repetition. My most important purpose has been to give a clear and consecutive account of what happened, because I believe that the story shows clearly the danger to which we are all exposed. It might have happened to you.

It is now just four weeks from the day of my last hearing before the Senate Subcommittee — four weeks so weary and so crowded that I have had little opportunity to know yet what so convulsive an ordeal has done to my personal life or to contemplate in impersonal detachment the meaning of such happenings in our national life. But I knew that if I did not sit down right away to tell the story of what happened, before allowing myself to begin the process of recovery, I would never do so. And of one thing I am convinced: it is important for as many people as possible to learn soon that "it can happen here."

The story would have been different, and more tragic, if it had not been for the law firm of Arnold, Fortas and Porter; and particularly for Abe Fortas, who after weeks of exhausting work on the "case" still had wisdom and patience left to give me counsel on the book.

Ruxton, Maryland
May 30, 1950

Ordeal by Slander

CHAPTER 1

It is cold in Afghanistan in March. All five members of the United Nations Technical Assistance Mission to Afghanistan were working in one crowded, smoky room around an iron stove that burned a lot of fuel but gave off little heat. There was some scuffling and whispering at the door and an Afghan messenger came in, bringing with him a blast of cold air that made everybody shout "Shut the door!" He brought me a telegram which read:

WASHINGTON 24 MARCH (RECEIVED KABUL 25 MARCH) SENATOR MC CARTHY SAYS OFF RECORD YOU TOP RUSSIAN ESPIONAGE AGENT IN UNITED STATES AND THAT HIS WHOLE CASE RESTS ON YOU STOP SAYS YOU STATE DEPARTMENT ADVISOR RECENTLY AS FOUR WEEKS AGO STOP HAVE CARRIED MRS. LATTIMORE'S AND DR. BRONK'S DENIALS OF MC CARTHY CHARGE AT PUBLIC SENATE HEARING THAT YOU PRO-COMMUNIST STOP PLEASE CABLE YOUR OWN COMMENT MC CARTHY'S ACCUSATIONS. BEALE ASSOCIATED PRESS.

My first reaction was an anger so hot and sweeping that it was hard to think. I walked away from the others, who were sorting out their own mail and telegrams, and studied the message. Then I got a piece of paper and drafted a reply, realizing that it would have to hit the front pages and hit them crisply. Clearly, this was going to be a fight to the finish, and a knockdown, drag-out fight. I had as yet no conception of the personality of McCarthy; but if he was a man who was willing to make a totally unfounded charge of espionage, this was going to be a dirty business.

Then I called over the other members of the mission. The telegram had been delivered through the Afghan Foreign Office, so the Afghan authorities would know all about it, and the members of my mission must be told about it too. Their reaction was prompt and strong: "That hysteria you people are having in America is going too far." They never for a moment doubted my loyalty. Neither did the Afghans, and thus there was never any question of breaking off the work of the mission.

I gave my reply to the mission secretary, a wonderful Canadian girl who took everything with unshaken calm, and she typed it out:

BEALE ASSOCIATED PRESS, WASHINGTON, D.C.

MC CARTHY'S OFF RECORD RANTINGS PURE MOONSHINE STOP DELIGHTED HIS WHOLE CASE RESTS ON ME AS THIS MEANS HE WILL FALL FLAT ON FACE STOP EXACTLY WHAT HE HAS SAID ON RECORD UNKNOWN HERE SO CANNOT REPLY IN DETAIL BUT WILL BE HOME IN FEW DAYS AND WILL CONTACT YOU THEN STOP

> OWEN LATTIMORE
> KABUL
> 25 MARCH 1950

Then I sat down to think.

The first I ever heard of Senator Joseph R. McCarthy, Republican of Wisconsin, had been just a few weeks before. While I was getting ready to go out to Afghanistan, the telephone rang one evening at my home in Ruxton, just outside of Baltimore. It was a long-distance call from a newspaperman in Denver, Colorado. He told me that Senator McCarthy was making a speech out there attacking the Department of State, and while he had not mentioned my name publicly, he had told newspapermen off the record that I was one of the people on his list. It didn't seem serious to me. Like many a citizen, I thought that attacking the Department of State in an election year was just another of those things. I told the newspaperman that Senator McCarthy was crazy if he had got me mixed up with the State Department. I had never been in the State Department. Then I finished up my preparations and went on out to Afghanistan.

But, like a dream that begins with something ridiculous and then branches and sprawls and crawls into horror and terror, the nightmare began to grow.

On March 14 I had received a telegram in Kabul from Reuters, the British news agency. It read:

SENATOR MC CARTHY IN SENATE FOREIGN RELATIONS SUB-COMMITTEE TODAY SAID YOU HAD COMMUNIST SYMPATHIES AND ADDED "THIS MAN'S RECORD AS PRO-COMMUNIST GOES BACK MANY YEARS." WE WOULD APPRECIATE ANY REPLY YOU CARE TO MAKE FOR PUBLICATION WORLD-WIDE AND ESPECIALLY IN AMERICA. WE HAVE ARRANGED FOR PRE-PAID REPLY UP TO 100 WORDS ADDRESSED PRESS REUTERS NEWS AGENCY LONDON.

There is no English-language newspaper in Kabul. The only Afghan newspaper, printed in Persian, is government-owned, and at that stage was not interested in telling the citizens of Kabul about Senator McCarthy. We had a radio where we were quartered, in a badly built "modern villa" on a magnificent avenue of poplar trees running far out beyond the edge of Kabul city; but half the time the current was so weak that the only stations we could get were New Delhi in India and Karachi in Pakistan, and these stations were so busy with propaganda quarrels between India and Pakistan and between Pakistan and Afghanistan that there was practically no world news. So I drove into town to see the American Ambassador.

I found him sympathetic. As far as the Embassy personnel were concerned, the attack on me was nothing but a trailer hooked onto attacks that McCarthy had already been making on Ambassador Philip C. Jessup, who had been in Kabul a few days before our United Nations Mission arrived. The Ambassador and all his staff were indignant about these attacks, which were extremely unsettling to American diplomacy at a time when Ambassador Jessup was making a survey trip all through Asia to look into the difficult problems of co-ordinating American policy.

Because of the lack of other news sources, the Embassy received regular telegrams summarizing American and world news. The file for the past few days was brought out and shown to me. It contained, of course, a great deal about McCarthy's charges against Ambassador Jessup.

There was a little bit, but not very much, about the charges against me. There was enough, however, for me to recognize the pattern immediately. These were charges that had been put out for years by Alfred C. Kohlberg and had been repeatedly disproved. I knew that Kohlberg, whom I had never met, was a millionaire fanatic who for years had spent a lot of money trying to work up pressure for all-out aid to Chiang Kai-shek.

Years ago Kohlberg had taken a violent dislike to the Institute of Pacific Relations, the leading American research institution dealing with the Far East. He had begun to build up a propaganda picture of the Institute as the evil genius of American policy in China, and of myself as one of the evil geniuses of the Institute. As an importer of laces and linens, Kohlberg had made a large part of his fortune out of China, where women and children, working for pitifully small wages, embroider linens for this trade. As a writer for the *China Monthly*, a magazine in Washington with Chinese Catholic associations, he is linked up with other protagonists of all-out aid to Chiang Kai-shek. He has contributed to the campaign funds of Senator Styles Bridges of New Hampshire, one of the congressional champions of unlimited intervention in China. He also founded his own magazine, *Plain Talk*, to which such people as Freda Utley have contributed. He is thus an important part of what has come to be known as the China Lobby, which also includes such people as William J. Goodwin, formerly a registered agent for the Chinese Government and still a consultant for the China Supply Commission, who was once prominent as a Christian Fronter.

The China Lobby also puts out its material through other pressure organizations. One of these is the Constitutional Educational League of Joseph P. Kamp. I later learned that Kamp's pamphlet "America Betrayed," which was distributed to members of Congress and editors all over the country just a week before McCarthy began his campaign, contained all the same charges against the same people in almost the same words. The Constitutional Educational League was one of the organizations named in the mass sedition indictments of 1942 and 1943 as a channel for propaganda tending to undermine the morale of the armed forces and thus "obstruct and defeat the war effort." Kamp himself was indicted by a Federal Grand Jury in 1944 when he refused to supply a list of contributors to his organization.

"This is the same old stuff all over again," I thought. "There's no use trying to deal with it by telegram from Kabul. A clear and simple statement when I get home will be all that's needed." I told the Ambassador the same thing, and decided not even to answer the telegram from Reuters.

On the fourteenth also I had received a telegram from Mr. Bert Andrews, Washington correspondent of the *New York Herald Tribune:*

SENATOR MC CARTHY HAS MADE SERIOUS CHARGES AGAINST YOUR LOYALTY STOP COULD YOU CABLE ME FIVE HUNDRED WORD STATEMENT COLLECT

To this I replied:

UNKNOWN HERE JUST WHAT MC CARTHY SAID THEREFORE DETAILED REPLY IMPOSSIBLE UNTIL RETURN IN FEW DAYS TIME WHEN WILL CONTACT YOU IN MEANTIME HOPE PUBLICITY WILL RESULT IN WIDE SALE MY BOOKS AND REALIZATION THAT COMMON SENSE IS POSSIBLE IN UNITED STATES FAR EASTERN POLICY.

From the fourteenth to the twenty-fifth I had heard nothing more of McCarthy. It was taking about two weeks for air mail to reach Kabul so letters from my wife were only full of news about work and plans at the Johns Hopkins University where she was taking over some of my work while I was away.

It was not possible, however, to forget the Associated Press telegram I received on March 25:

SENATOR MC CARTHY SAYS OFF RECORD YOU TOP RUSSIAN ESPIONAGE AGENT IN UNITED STATES.

If that charge had been made off the record, every newspaper in America would know about it already. When would it break into print? With the little that I had to go on, I tried to figure out the situation.

1. The charge was the kind of lie that followed the Goebbels formula of the big lie: a lie so big that a lot of people would say: "He couldn't make an accusation like that with nothing to back it up. There must be something in it."

2. The time factor was important. How many days were there going to be for building up and adorning the lie? By the time I got home, how far would McCarthy have been able to succeed in building up a false and distorted picture of me in the public mind?

3. A big lie of this kind would not stand just by itself. Clearly, I faced the danger of supplementary lies. Perhaps it would go as far as perjured evidence. I would have to face that possibility. (I had yet to learn that McCarthy is a master not only of the big lie but of the middle-sized lie and the little ball-bearing lie that rolls around and around and helps the wheels of the lie machinery to turn over.)

On one thing, however, I was determined. I must not let the attack on me cut short my stay in Afghanistan by a single day. If I dropped my work and hurried home, it would harm the United Nations mission to Afghanistan, and it would certainly be a terrible blow to American prestige. American relations both with the Afghan Government and with the United Nations program of technical aid were extremely cordial. United Nations technical aid to Afghanistan would combine very well with American Point Four aid for a program of development.

My decision to stay was fortified by a cordial telegram from the United Nations saying that the Secretary General had sent a message to the Afghanistan representative to the United Nations pointing out that my appointment as the Secretary General's special representative to discuss with the Government of Afghanistan the organization of a United Nations mission of technical assistance to Afghanistan was based on the Secretary General's conviction that in view of my long-standing international reputation as an expert concerning economic, social and cultural problems of Asia I would perform my duties in the best interests of Afghanistan and of the United Nations, and stating that he continued to hold this view.

There was a lot at stake. Accordingly, I put the ugly situation waiting for me at home out of my mind, as far as possible, and followed through on my mission. We concluded an agreement that was thoroughly satisfactory both to the United Nations and to the Afghan Government, and then, on the day originally planned, and not a day earlier, we left Kabul.

It is a full day's drive, long and tiring, through the magnificent mountains of Afghanistan down to the Khyber Pass, up and over the Pass, through its fortifications, and on down to Peshawar in the wide plains of Pakistan. The mission was completed, and I began to brood over my own problems, but there was no news at Peshawar. No mail, no telegrams, nothing in the newspaper, nothing on the radio. I had expected that, but even so it meant another twenty-four hours of darkness, turning things over and over in my mind without new material to refresh my thinking. One important thing was not to let myself get tense and on edge. I turned in early and slept well.

The next day we flew to Karachi. There seemed to be "technical difficulties." We spent a long time at one of the intermediate stops, where mechanics fiddled with the plane. We got into Karachi very late at night. The "technical difficulties" apparently included trouble with the plane's radio, so that when we finally landed, our plane had not been heard from for several hours. I was glad that no lurid alarm had been flashed back to America to add to my wife's worries. The only newspaperman at the airport was a representative of United Press. He very considerately brought along a file of incoming news. I contented myself with a brief and, I hoped, effective repetition of my denial of the McCarthy charges.

The airfield at Karachi lies miles out in the desert. We were traveling by a British airline. I found out that mail and telegrams addressed to me in care of this line might be delivered either at the airfield, at the hostel for passengers where we were staying half a mile or so from the airfield, or at two widely separated offices of the company in the city. In addition, some letters and telegrams might of course have been addressed to me in care of the American Embassy. The situation was saved by my companions of the United Nations — an Englishman, a Canadian, and an

Australian. All three were men who had seen a lot of the world. They knew that the Communist problem is a serious problem, but important and comforting for me was the fact that, having worked closely with me on economic problems that had all kinds of political and social ramifications, they knew perfectly well that I do not have a mind like a Communist. Their support and consideration were wonderful. They were ready to talk when I wanted to talk, and let me alone when they could see that I wanted to be left alone. These three men went off in various directions to look for my mail.

In the meantime, I was free to go into town and call at the Embassy. The Ambassador, a fellow Marylander, Mr. Avra Warren, took me out for a quiet and restful lunch with his wife. Most of the afternoon I spent reading the New York papers, delivered to the Embassy by air mail. The latest were only about three days old.

All of the Embassy staff were naturally more concerned about the way the McCarthy charges were disrupting the work of our diplomatic service and lowering its prestige than they were about my fate as an individual. I also saw several old Pakistani friends, one of them a man who had served in China and was an expert on the Chinese Moslems. Among Americans and Pakistanis alike, the reaction was just what it had been in Kabul. They had not heard much about the attack on me, but they knew all about the attack on Ambassador Jessup. There was a general feeling of dismay. Nobody wanted to see the spread of Communism in Asia. Nobody wanted to see more countries coming under the shadow of Russian power. The Americans in Kabul and in Karachi liked the people of the countries they were working in, and wanted to work with them. The Afghans and the Pakistanis wanted co-operation with the United States to be as close and cordial as possible, consistent with maintaining their own political independence and freedom of initiative in economic matters. But they were dismayed by the impression of political chaos in Washington. They were convinced that the best way to make themselves immune both to Communist infiltration and to Russian pressure was to build up and modernize their countries. But they were frightened of the idea of being put in the front line of the cold war against Russia when, with the news coming from America, they felt more and more that American backing might be feeble, hesitant, and crippled by an irresponsible and fantastic civil war among American congressmen and senators.

Eventually I got all my mail and telegrams in reverse order — the most recent letters and telegrams first, and the earlier messages last. The final batch was not delivered until just as we were getting aboard the plane. So it was not until we were in flight that I was able to sort things out and start on the big thinking job that lay ahead.

One letter from my wife, dated March 23, said:

Oh darling, this probably won't reach you before you leave — but I'll try anyway. I have just learned that the matter is *much* more serious than I had thought — about as serious as possible — but it is so utterly fantastic and incredible that it may be easier to disprove. Fewer people will believe. It seems like a nightmare. They have absolutely nothing to go on but the calumny of your enemies, but I don't know how far they may have gone in manufacturing evidence. . . .

I'm going to consult Abe Fortas tomorrow. . . . I'm not being as hysterical as this sounds — I just want to get this off in a hurry on the off chance of reaching you. I'll write everything to London.

I never loved you more, darling. I'm sure you'll handle it wonderfully.

I'm saying nothing.

All my love, and faith. Hurry home!

Then there was a brief note dated March 26:

Darling — no time for a letter — Drew Pearson really broke the story tonight. Papers will probably have it tomorrow. He gave you terrific support.

So that was what I had to go on. As the plane droned on through the night, I thought first and most of Eleanor. I felt very selfish. The first impact of the news on me, in the almost unbelievable remoteness of Afghanistan, had been very narrow and personal, driving me in on myself. I realized that I had been taking for granted not only Eleanor's courage and devotion, but her competence as an organizer and chief of staff. Of course she had been getting together everything needed for my defense and doing a superbly efficient job of it. Of course she had taken legal advice, and undoubtedly good advice. But what about all the loneliness and worry she had been going through and would still have to go through up to the moment I landed?

It was easier for me. At first my anger had been boiling hot. By now it had grown cold and sharp-edged. Sitting in the plane and thinking, what I had to do was to analyze the reasons for that anger, and to organize the anger itself, turning it into an effective weapon not simply for defense, but for counterattack against this McCarthy, whoever he might turn out to be. But I was like a soldier coming up from the rear, getting ready for battle. Eleanor was already in the front line, wondering desperately when the reinforcements would come up.

Then I thought, or tried to think, about Abe Fortas. I remembered that I had once met him at somebody's house at dinner, and that I had had an impression of him as a man with a keen mind and a warm and human personality. But I found that I could not fit him into my thinking as my own lawyer, helping me to defend my own case. Never having been involved in any kind of legal proceedings, I had a vague feeling that most lawyers are fixers rather than fighters. This fellow McCarthy was obviously a roundhouse brawler and a dirty fighter. A fight with him would be a slugging match. I was all set to slug, but was Abe Fortas going to be the kind of lawyer who would try to make me pull my punches?

With what Eleanor had written, and what I had read in the New York papers at the Embassy, I could see more clearly what kind of fight it was going to be. Obviously, there was much more to it than an unjustified attack on an individual by an irresponsible senator. I was not a State Department advisor, but he was not calling me a State Department advisor just out of ignorance. He was using me as an excuse to attack the China policy of the State Department; through the State Department, evidently, he was hoping to throw the Administration off balance in an election year. The wording of the charges against me made it clear that he was relying on the China Lobby to help him put up a smoke screen.

I knew why I had already been sniped at by the China Lobby. It was because I had enough firsthand knowledge to form independent judgments. I was not a captive of the Chiang Kai-shek line, the China Lobby line, the State Department line, or the Old China Hand line. The China Lobby wanted a simplified propaganda picture of China with all-out supporters of Chiang Kai-shek lined up on one side, Communists on the other side, and nobody allowed in the middle. Independents like myself must be cleared out of the middle of the picture because we knew what we were talking about and because people read our books and articles. The simplest way to clear us out would be by the kind of double-flank attack indicated by the McCarthy charges — calling us Communists and at the same time accusing us of close connections with the State Department.

I was beginning to realize now that what made these tactics possible was the deepening atmosphere of uncertainty, suspicion, and divided opinion in America. The charges themselves were flimsy, but they were taking advantage of — and at the same time contributing to — an increasingly nervous and panicky public opinion. Even the "top Russian espionage agent" charge was not something to be laughed off just because of its outrageous falsity. For a long time now fear of spies had been feeding fear of Communist subversion, and fear of Communism had been building up fear of espionage.

With nervous fear abroad in the land, it might be easy to smear a man like me who had worked for years in China and in other countries in which Communism had become increasingly important. My colleagues in the university world knew I was no Communist. So did the top men in the newspaper world — especially the top Far Eastern correspondents. So did the State Department people — especially those dealing with China and the rest of Asia.

But if I could be intimidated, or if people could be frightened out of having anything to do with me, it would be a long step toward successful intimidation of all university research and teaching, of the free expression of opinion in the press and on the radio, and of the State Department in its dealings with all independent specialists and consultants. I had better make up my mind, therefore, that this attack was not going to be just guerrilla warfare. It was going to be an all-out effort to knock me out of circulation and to terrorize others.

We had expected to make a refueling stop in Iraq, but plans were changed while in flight, and we kept right on going till we hit Cairo. Perhaps because of this change, there were no newspapermen at the Cairo airport. We took off again and flew to Rome. As we taxied to a stop, I could see a lot of photographers and newsmen. "You're in for it now," said one of my companions. "It's going to be like this all the rest of the way home." All the passengers looked at me curiously, and made way for me to go out ahead and alone. It was the beginning of a feeling of being a target that was not to leave me for many weeks. This kind of experience, when you are not used to it, tightens up your nerves and makes you tense and wary. You are constantly on the watch for something that rarely happens, but is very dangerous when it does happen — an "angled" question that is intended to trap you into saying something that can be played up against you, to make you look like a suspicious character. When that happens, it makes you very angry, but you have to keep your temper and answer calmly and frankly, straightening out the issue, whatever it is.

From Rome we flew direct to London. One thing worried me: how to get a chance to see my mail and telegrams before meeting the newspapermen. In making a statement through the press, I did not want to be evasive. Yet how could I say anything to them, when they would obviously know much more than I did, unless I could first have a look at all the press clippings and other material that Eleanor would certainly have waiting for me?

I need not have worried. The British authorities handled everything with the unruffled calm that only the British appear to be able to summon up when everything is going haywire. The top people in authority around the airfield — most of them I never did identify individually, and I am sorry, because I felt very grateful to them — were waiting for me. Like a character in a novel of international intrigue, I was whisked aside from the rest of the passengers, and taken into an empty room that I was afterwards told was known as the V.I.P. room.

That was the only moment of mystery. From then on the whole atmosphere was one of the friendliest understanding. Nobody said it, but from every face I could read the expression "what these crazy Americans do to their own people is a caution!" My mail and telegrams were brought in to me. Various people took charge of the business of taking my health card, passport, and baggage to the right places to get the right stamps put on them. I talked on the telephone to the United Nations Office in London.

They had sent a man all the way to the airfield with mail for me. I was told that a telephone call from Washington was coming through for me, from Abe Fortas, and while waiting for it I read my mail.

Of course the first letter I read was one from Eleanor, written partly on March 24 and partly on March 25. It began: **14459**

My darling, I don't know if I'm in Moscow or the moon. It certainly isn't the United States. I have heard more fantastic and terrifying things in the last twenty-four hours than could happen in a nightmare. I haven't time to go into details now because I want to get this mailed tonight so it will surely reach you. . . .

If you heard everything in Karachi and got my last messy note, you have been having a pretty ghastly journey and I know what has been going round and round in your mind. You are going to have an opportunity of a lifetime to affect the future of democracy in this country. McCarthy has staked everything now on this one case, so that if he is thoroughly demolished now his whole house of cards tumbles and his methods and all he stands for fall with them. I am too tired to express myself sensibly, but all your friends and all the decent people in America are backing you and counting on you to come out with flying colors. You will have saved the 81 people on his State Department list, and a lot of other people who will soon be on other lists if he gets by with this. (Possibly some of the 81 shouldn't be saved, but you will have saved the good and the innocent.)

I know you have been thinking of how you can make your defense not only an offensive against McCarthy, which is absolutely necessary, but how you can make a really great positive statement, about your own life and your country and democracy and peace and freedom — and make it without sounding too starry-eyed and "unrealistic," because these are tough guys you'll be talking to and the reporters who will interpret it to the public are tough. Some of them are saying that these McCarthy attacks are good for the country, that a lot of people should be purged, etc.

Next, I read a letter from Abe Fortas and had my first clear indication of his mind and personality in a short but crystal-clear summary of everything that had happened and everything that had been done since my wife had consulted him and his partners. I quote just a few paragraphs:

As evidence of your non-Communist attitude, Pearson broke at some length the story of the Living Buddha and the two other Mongols who are in residence at the University. The result of this has been a great press demand for interviews with them. With much hesitation, and only because it seemed necessary, an interview has been arranged for 4:30 this afternoon. One of my associates is in Baltimore now preparing this interview, and I think that it will go well, and without too great an imposition upon the three persons concerned. The emphasis in this part of the story will be that these people are refugees from Communism who were brought to this country as a result of your efforts and who are and will be of great assistance in contributing to an understanding of the Far Eastern problem. This may sound somewhat insane to you, but I assure you that we are operating in a situation characterized by insanity, and a certain amount of drama is not only desirable, but also completely unavoidable. You will realize that every newspaper in the country has assigned its top men to this story and that they will leave no angle unexplored. . . .

It may be necessary that you get down in the gutter in which we are now operating as a result of Senator McCarthy's personal attack on you. But if we can place the Senator in the gutter where he belongs before your return, it may be that the best strategy, both from your personal viewpoint and in terms of the national interest, will be for you to address yourself in your statements before the Senate Committee to the underlying issues which have made possible this attack upon you. . . . We hope that, primarily as a result of Mrs. Lattimore's work, we will have your own material and the charges that have been made against you so prepared that you will be able within the shortest possible time to prepare your statement for the Committee after your return here.

Again, I want to say for myself, Thurman, and Paul, that we are glad to be in the fight on your side, and to express our hope that you will not consider that we have been presumptuous in taking the action that has been taken to date or which we shall undoubtedly have to take in the next few days on your behalf.

Enclosed were letters signed separately by Arnold, Fortas and Porter that they had written to Senator Tydings, Chairman of the Subcommittee of the Senate Foreign Relations Committee before which I should appear, and to Senator McCarthy. The letter to Senator Tydings summarized the situation to date and went on:

Meanwhile, great damage is being done to Mr. Lattimore and to the nation's interest in his unique ability to contribute to the fight against the spread of Communism in the Far East. In order to minimize this damage, we are completing an analysis of all of Mr. Lattimore's publications and writings which are available to us. We shall, as soon as possible, forward our summaries to your Committee and shall make them available to the press and the public. We have also collected Mr. Lattimore's private files, as well as his published works, and we request that your Committee direct its investigators to examine these documents. Mrs. Lattimore and ourselves will be available to your investigators or to members of your Committee to supply any and all information concerning Mr. Lattimore's views and activities which you may desire.

We are confident that you and the members of your Committee are fully aware of the national and individual values that are here at stake. We have no doubt that if the facts concerning Mr. Lattimore receive publicity comparable to the scurrilous charges against him, the American people will realize that he is a patriot and that his accusers are character assassins who seek what appears to them temporary partisan advantage in reckless disregard of the national welfare.

We are enclosing, for the information of your Committee, copy of a letter that we have today sent to Senator McCarthy.

The letter to McCarthy I read, naturally, with a specially keen interest. It showed me, to my immense relief, that my lawyers were not going to rely on passive defense. The last paragraph read:

We write this letter to you at this time to give you an opportunity publicly to retract and repudiate your charges that Mr. Lattimore is a Communist or Communist sympathizer or the agent of a foreign power. We suggest that a decent regard for the welfare of your country, for the high office that you hold, and for elementary Christian values, require you immediately to put a stop to this fantastic outrage. We are required, however, to inform you that any withdrawal of your charges that you now make will not, as a matter of law, exonerate you from such legal liability as you may have in the event that Mr. Lattimore chooses to bring action against you for the statements that you have made concerning him, including your "off-the-record" identification of him as the person whom you libelously accuse of being the "top Soviet espionage agent."

Then I went out to face the flashbulbs and talk to the reporters. One thing I noticed right away. Not only the English reporters, but also the Americans were quite obviously assuming that I was innocent until proved guilty. Among the newspapermen in the group at London airport was Hamilton Owens, editor of the *Baltimore Sun*. The fact that he had come all the way to London to meet me was like getting a signal in a code to which I had the key. I knew that the *Baltimore Sun*, as my home-town paper, would be exposed to the full pressure of unreasoning emotion as soon as the McCarthy charges against me came out. I also knew that the editorial page of the paper had a tendency to be flabby. I had therefore guessed that as soon as the sensational McCarthy charges had come into the open, the *Sun* had played the news on its front page with the biggest headlines that the printing room could provide while hesitating, on its editorial page, to point out that in my own university and my own community my loyalty has never been doubted. (They later sent a man up to Wisconsin who wrote some good stories on McCarthy.)

I could therefore see right away that at least one of the reasons why Hamilton Owens had come all the way to London was that he was looking for a safe way to write a friendly story about me. This he did, and I was very grateful to him for it. He described me as being angry but not afraid, and added the nice human touch that when I was tired I relaxed and slept "the sleep of the just." He also gave me some very good advice about the obvious fact that the charges against me were going to be tried by newspaper as much as by the processes of a senatorial sub-committee.

I had a leisurely dinner with Hamilton Owens, and we boarded the plane that was to take us to New York and flew as far as Shannon, Ireland, where we were held over-night, and I got a beautiful sleep in a comfortable bed. Shannon is my favorite airport in the world. When you land there, before you get off the plane, a girl comes aboard and says, in a brogue that has to be heard to be believed, "Ye're now in Oireland," and I always wonder why the passengers are such a stuffy and unimaginative lot that they don't burst out cheering. The waiting room and dining room are bright and cheerful, the grass outside is an Irish green, the waiters all have a lovely soft County Clare way of talking, and they serve you the best bacon and eggs in the world and beefsteaks that are really beefsteaks.

I felt myself tensing up again as we approached New

York. It is a dreadful thing to come home from halfway across the world, knowing that although people in other countries have been sympathetic and understanding, you may be met in your own country either by hostility, because of a campaign of slander, or by people who are afraid to greet you frankly, because they have been scared off by a campaign of intimidation. I did know, however, exactly what I wanted to do when we landed. I knew I would be met by reporters who would want, not a full statement, but something that could be flashed quickly to the wire services and the newspapers. I therefore wanted to get that over with quickly, and then have a chance to consult with Eleanor, and with Abe Fortas if he was there, before making a more formal statement.

When we landed, at five in the morning, and I came down the steps, the massing of cameramen was like a line of European sportsmen with shotguns waiting for pheasant to be driven in by beaters who have been whacking the bushes. They were not satisfied when I came down the steps and they all flashed their bulbs at me as I passed, but wanted me to go back up and do it over again. This I thought a little bit too much, so I said something vague and, I hope, polite and hurried on into the waiting room. No special consideration here, as at London. I waited like the others until my name was called, and went through the routine formalities. The only exception was that Abe Fortas and a man from United Nations were allowed to come in and speak to me before I left the customs shed to go out and face the reporters and the newsreel cameras.

When I came out, there was Eleanor. I rushed to give her a hug and a kiss, and a press camera flashed, getting a picture of me with my eyes popping out and my mouth open, and a general expression resembling a hungry polar bear about to pounce on a sleek seal. Then I looked around, and there was David, our nineteen-year-old son, who had come down from Harvard. Then I had to speak to the newspapermen. I made it short and pithy, calling McCarthy "base and despicable." In front of the newsreel cameras I repeated my opinion of McCarthy, putting into it all the anger and contempt that I felt. Then they hustled me into a United Nations car, and we drove into town, where a friend had put an apartment at our disposal. After a quick bath and change into clean clothes, we went around to the St. Moritz Hotel for breakfast with Abe Fortas so that we could work together in preparation for the press conference which had been scheduled for that afternoon.

When we had finished up the statement and sent it out to be mimeographed for distribution to the press we lunched on sandwiches and then went down to the press conference. A friend of Abe Fortas's, in a public relations firm, had arranged for a big room in the hotel. As we came in and I saw the banks of powerful lights and newsreel cameras, a thought flashed through the back of my mind. I wondered what kind of money this was running into. But neither Abe nor Eleanor had yet said a word about money, and I wasn't going to. This thing was bigger than money.

I sat down and read my statement which was short and concentrated on three things: that, far from being the "architect of Far Eastern Policy," I have in fact had no influence on the drafting of American Far Eastern policy; that I am not and never have been a Communist, have never advocated the Communist cause, and have no Communist connections; and finally, that I am an independent expert and commentator and throughout my career have never hesitated to criticize official policy whenever, according to my knowledge and my conscience, I have thought that was the right thing to do. In this connection, ever since the surrender of Japan in 1945 I have been convinced, and many people have agreed with me, that if only the State Department had in fact adopted some of my ideas, and adopted them early enough, China would not today be in the hands of the Communists, and the structure of American policy and American interests all over Asia would not be in such a mess.

The questions were friendly. I could see that the reporters were making up their minds that I was an honest and innocent man, falsely accused in a sensational orgy of dirty politics. Almost all the reporters were strangers to me, and that made it all the nicer when big, burly Bob Cochrane of the *Baltimore Sun*, whom I had known in Tokyo, pushed his way to the front to shake hands and wish me luck.

Abe took care of one more detail. He sent a telegram to Budenz, asking him in the interests of fair play either to disavow the press rumor that he had signed an affidavit for McCarthy or, if he had, to advise us immediately and to disclose its contents. No answer ever came.

Then Eleanor and I went down to Baltimore by train. This was Saturday. We were going to have Sunday to rest at home, and then go over to Washington on Monday and prepare for my hearing before the Senate Subcommittee. I was more tired than I had realized — tired right down into my bones, and I slept all the way to Baltimore. David and his tall, red-headed friend, Emily Lewis, had gone by an earlier train. They had done the week-end marketing, and were ready to meet us and drive us out to our home in Ruxton. When we got there and were greeted by Carrie, who has been with us since David was a child and is one of the family, it seemed that nothing in the world could be more peaceful than the little house under its tall trees.

But Sunday was not a day of rest. I read McCarthy's speech, which had taken him more than four hours to deliver and I realized that McCarthyism is not a thing to be fixed, it is an octopus to be fought. Psychologically, the very fact that I was innocent made the whole nightmare more paralyzing. The charges against me built up a circumstantial picture of a man who might have existed. I was not that man, but those were the charges I had to refute. If I was not careful, I might fall into a trap. People might think I was trying to defend myself against real charges.

In the intervals Eleanor prepared materials to take over to Washington, and told me the story of what had been happening while I was in Afghanistan. Here is her story.

CHAPTER 11

BY ELEANOR LATTIMORE

I HAD STAYED at home until after the mail came, hoping for a letter from Owen, so did not get down to his office until late on the morning of March 13. He is the director of the Page School of International Relations at the Johns Hopkins University. He had flown to Afghanistan just a week before, and every day I had been going in to the office to tend to his mail and other chores I often did for him when he was away. On this particular day Hall Paxton, who had just returned from Sinkiang where he had been American Consul, and several other people were coming over from the State Department to visit our Inner Asian seminar, and I had invited some Hopkins people to have lunch with them first at the Faculty Club.

Before they arrived I was called to the telephone. A reporter at the *Baltimore Evening Sun* wanted me to comment on the report that Joseph McCarthy had named my husband as a "pro-Communist" advisor to the State Department. My comment was that it was ridiculous. He was not pro-Communist but anti-Communist, and he had no connection with the State Department. I suggested that the accusation sounded like ones that had been made against him several years ago when he had begun to criticize the Nationalist Government of China. At that time it was easy to label critics of that government as pro-Communist, but my husband had criticized it exactly because he felt its policies were strengthening Communism in China. One after another, reporters and wire services called and I said the same to all of them. Since my husband had never been connected with the State Department it seemed pointless to include him in the attack. I was foolish enough to believe that when McCarthy discovered his mistake he would move on to other prey. But I wished that Owen were anywhere but in Afghanistan, so he could dispose of the nasty business quickly.

By mid-afternoon the early editions of the evening papers were brought in and I was horrified to see screaming headlines across the tops of both the *Evening Sun* and the Baltimore Hearst paper, the *News-Post*, "McCARTHY CALLS LATTIMORE 3 OTHERS PRO–RED AT PROBE!" "LATTIMORE BAD RISK TYDINGS PROBERS TOLD." Both papers had printed my denials on the front page beside their stories of the accusations, but the sensational headlines obscured the effect of fair play. The Hearst headlines, incidentally, were smaller and less sensational than the *Sun's*. The details of McCarthy's speech, which had not been received by the papers at the time they had asked me for comment, made me begin to realize the seriousness of the charges. They were all either complete lies or such distortions of fact as to have the effect of complete lies. They were ridiculously false, yet how were people who didn't know my husband to know that they were false? Afghanistan seemed farther away than ever.

Since it would be days, perhaps weeks, before Owen could reply for himself it seemed to me that something should be said, either by me, or preferably by the university. I telephoned immediately to ask for an appointment with Dr. Bronk, the president and went to see him at six o'clock.

The same evening I telephoned to a friend at the United Nations to ask if he could find out for me if any steps would be taken to inform Owen of the attack which had been made upon him. He let me know the next day that a long cable was being sent, and also that strong messages of continued confidence in him were being sent to the Afghanistan Embassy for transmission to their government. Owing to cumbersome United Nations machinery, however, and slowness of communications, the cable did not reach Owen for a week.

I had explained to Dr. Bronk that McCarthy's accusations all stemmed from the attempts of the Chinese Nationalists to destroy by any means anyone who criticized the Kuomintang. I also told him that I would give him a memorandum of the facts about each accusation.

I spent several nights working on this memorandum. I could work very little in the daytime because all day long the telephone rang. Dozens of friends from Baltimore, Washington, New York, even as far away as California, rang up to commiserate, encourage, advise and discuss. I was very glad they did, but it took most of my time, so that it was difficult to accumulate the information I needed, from files and friends, to prepare the memorandum.

As I pointed out in the letter I sent to Dr. Bronk enclosing this memorandum, all but one of McCarthy's charges were duplicates of those made by Alfred Kohlberg in his attack on the Institute of Pacific Relations in 1947. Kohlberg had been completely discredited at that time, and I was exasperated to have to go to so much trouble to look up the data all over again to answer his really silly charges. The one new charge was a three-word quotation taken entirely out of context and made to mean something entirely different from what was actually said.

I wanted to send a copy of this memorandum to Senator Tydings, but Owen's good friend Stewart Macaulay, the provost of the university, and several others whom I consulted, urged me not to. I agreed with them then that a wife's answers wouldn't mean very much and that it was better to wait, but I believe now I should have sent it. Four out of five members of the committee would have given it fair consideration which might have mitigated the effects of the next attack. It was Owen's remoteness and his long silence which enabled McCarthy to renew and enlarge his assault.

On March 21 I finally had word that Owen had arrived in Kabul and had received the United Nations cable. He replied to the United Nations that he planned to leave Kabul March 27 after completing his mission there and would deal with the charges immediately upon his return. I had already suggested to Mr. Macaulay that the university request a hearing for him, and he had drafted a letter for Dr. Bronk to sign. There had been a delay in sending it, with the result that on the twenty-second it was reported in the *Sun* that in answer to a query Senator Tydings had said that Owen Lattimore had not requested a hearing. I then immediately wrote a letter to Tydings myself, asking for a hearing, and a friend took it over to him in Washington.

One person I did send my memorandum to was Philip Jessup. Dr. Jessup had been in Paris when McCarthy began to accuse him of "having a special affinity for Communist causes." He cabled a denial and flew home earlier than he had intended in order to answer the charges in person. At a press conference on March 22 McCarthy had called Jessup "the voice of Lattimore," saying also, "Everything that Jessup has done so far in the East has been a case where the voice is Jessup's but the hand is Lattimore's." This was ridiculous, of course. Owen had known Phil Jessup for seventeen years, chiefly through the Institute of Pacific Relations, but Jessup had always been senior to him and there was never any question of trying to "influence" him.

It seemed to me at that time that because of Dr. Jessup's eminence and skill he was the one who would be able to stem McCarthy's wild character-assassinations, and that the fate of many of the fifty-seven or eighty-one State Department people he was accusing of being Communists was in his hands — and perhaps my husband's fate too. I wrote him something to this effect, since it seemed to me most probable that Owen's name would come up in Dr. Jessup's hearing, and that they would naturally benefit by defending each other. It did come up, and many of our mutual friends told me of their disappointment that he did not make some sort of an affirmative statement of the belief in Owen's integrity and loyalty which I'm sure he had.

The staff and students in the Page School of International Relations, of which my husband is director, were almost as angry and indignant as I was about McCarthy's accusations, and eager to do something. I wanted to prepare some material which I thought Owen might need at his hearing, and suggested to some of them that they go through his writings and his files to find passages and letters which would show clearly he was not pro-Communist, and to others that they go through Alfred Kohlberg's writings to show how close his earlier charges were to McCarthy's. It made us all feel better to be able to work, and there was plenty to do, since Owen has been an appallingly prolific author for more than twenty years.

On Thursday, March 23 I was having lunch with Maggie Kahin, whose husband George is on the staff of the Page School, when the telephone rang. Mr. Kirkpatrick of the *San Francisco Chronicle* wanted to know when my husband was coming home. I told him the first of April. Then he said, "I suppose you have heard about the charges." I thought he was being funny, and remarked that I had been hearing nothing else for ten days. "No," he said, "I mean the new ones, that he is the top Russian spy in this country." My heart turned over.

For several days McCarthy had been boasting that he had given to the Senate investigating committee the name of "the top Russian espionage agent in this country," whom he had described as the "former boss of Alger Hiss" in an "espionage ring in the Department." The night before I had heard a report on the radio that Senator Tydings had said that the man McCarthy had named had no connection with the State Department except that five years ago he had been on a mission abroad, that once he had given a lecture to State Department employees and on another occasion had taken part in a two-day round-table conference. McCarthy had replied, "This is completely untrue. This man has a desk at the State Department and has access to the files, at least he had until four or five weeks ago. He is one of the top advisors on Far Eastern affairs, has been for a long time and they know it." Nothing in McCarthy's description fitted Owen, but the thought crossed my mind that Tydings's description did. He had been on the Reparations Mission to Japan five years ago. It was a White House mission, but I had just discovered in looking through old records that he had been paid by the State Department. But the thought was too fantastic. He didn't know any Russians in this country, or any Communists. He didn't have access to any secret material. How could *anybody*, even McCarthy, accuse him of being a spy?

Joe Barnes, one of Owen's closest and oldest friends, and his wife had stopped for the night at our house on their way south. Joe had been seeing newspapermen in New York. Everyone was speculating about the identity of the mysterious spy. No one had mentioned Owen. I decided I was getting neurotic. Joe had been reassuring, but the last thing he said before they had left that morning was that he would come back if I needed him. Now I knew that I needed him. I hastily telephoned to Washington, where the Barneses were having lunch on their way south, and they said they would wait for me.

By the time I got to Washington Joe had discovered that two days before Senator McCarthy had called a press conference and told some newspapermen, off the record, that the No. 1 spy he had been talking about was Owen Lattimore. None of them had printed it for fear of libel, but the story was all over Washington. The Barneses had taken a room at the Hotel Willard, and I managed to get the only other one available, a dreary little room-without-bath for which I had to pay in advance because I had no baggage. After dinner Joe went out to see what else he could learn.

I don't know how I happened to think of Abe Fortas, because everybody in Washington knew more about him than I did. We had met him once at dinner, and heard him talking about the attack on Dr. Condon and the way in which he thought such attacks should be handled. Owen and I had both liked what he said but, not dreaming that my husband ever would be in a similar situation, I had not given Mr. Fortas another thought. So it was instinct rather than cleverness that made me telephone him that night to ask for an appointment. When he told me he would see me at ten o'clock the next morning I somehow felt much better. I got a hasty letter off to Owen which I hoped might reach him in Karachi on his way home, bought some toilet articles at a drug store, and went to bed.

At breakfast Joe told us an incredible story. He had gone to a party where there were a lot of people, and there, of all people, he had met McCarthy. I had been thinking of McCarthy as the embodiment of all the powers of darkness and not as someone a friend of mine could meet at a party. For days I had been living in an unreal and fantastic hell. Somehow the fact that Joe had seen and talked with the Devil jolted me into a realization that the Devil was a reality. Joe had tried to convince him that he couldn't be more wrong about Jessup and Lattimore. Others at the party were telling the Senator that he was crazy. But he had seemed completely unshakable. From others Joe had heard incredible stories about the methods by which McCarthy planned to substantiate his charges. It was very frightening.

Joe was finally convinced it was going to be tough, and he and Betty approved of my talking with Mr. Fortas. They promised to wait until after I had seen him, though they were already way behind their schedule of important engagements. I went alone to see him. Strange to say it was the first time I had ever been in a lawyer's office. But in the sea of unreality in which I had been floundering I knew at once that Abe Fortas was another solid rock, like Joe and Betty. I hadn't been there ten minutes before I knew that going to see him was the wisest thing I'd ever done. He immediately grasped, far better than I had, how serious the situation was. My husband might be named publicly at any moment as the top Russian espionage agent in the United States. He knew how vital it was to be ready to act promptly — to demand that McCarthy retract his charges, to demand that a government plane be sent out to bring Owen home immediately, to make his personal files and all his writings available to the investigating committee, to feed material about him to the press. It was breath-taking. I knew he was right but I was afraid to take so much responsibility. I sent for Joe. Mr. Fortas brought in his partners, Thurman Arnold and Paul Porter. Listening to the three of them, Joe was as sure as I was that they were right. A great burden had been lifted from my shoulders. Joe and Betty continued south, feeling that they were leaving Owen's problem in the best possible hands.

I had been so sure these men would help me that I didn't realize until after I had left them that their decision was greater than mine. They could so easily have told me that they were too busy. I had taken them on faith, but they had taken Owen on faith. I needed them desperately, and they didn't need Owen at all. And yet they hadn't hesitated a minute. The only question they asked about Owen was, "Will he fight?" I knew he would fight, but how could they know? It is faith that moves mountains, and there were mountains to move.

There was still at least a week before Owen could be home. I went back to our house in the country north of Baltimore to pack all the things we would need. At a newsstand in the railway station I bought the *New York Journal-American* because I saw a story on the front page which pointed out that the description of the mysterious "Mr. X" fitted Owen Lattimore. It was six o'clock when I got to the house. I turned on the radio to hear Eric Sevareid mentioning Owen's name. He was saying, too, that the description fitted Owen Lattimore.

Two minutes after the program ended Mr. Sevareid telephoned to ask if I had been listening to what he had just said about Owen. He said he was afraid it would have worried me but the report was already so widespread that he thought it was bound to be made public very soon. I spent almost all night packing into the car Owen's files and all the things I could find that he had ever written. Unfortunately the Lattimores are not very systematic about keeping magazine and newspaper articles, and it was quite a job assembling them all. A good friend came out to help me. We found copies of his eleven books, in various editions and languages, and eight others to which he had contributed a chapter or a long introduction. We found about eighty magazine articles, some in his study, some in file drawers, and some in cartons in the garage, and we found files of hundreds of syndicated newspaper articles he had written for Overseas News Agency.

Early the next morning I started back to Washington with everything in the car. I hated to leave our peaceful house, just as the early spring bulbs were beginning to blossom. There were already drifts of daffodils and narcissus along the edge of the woods. And I hated to leave sixty-four-year old Carrie Thomas all alone, the good friend who had looked after us for many years. She disliked staying alone at night. She hated the telephone. She was terribly disturbed and baffled by what was happennig. But for weeks after that morning she faced everything with sturdy loyalty — the telephone that rang day and night, the newspapermen who tried to force their way into the house, the questioning and all the unknown terrors — and the few times we were able to come home during the long ordeal she was always ready to make a haven for us and any number of friends and helpers we might bring along.

I knew I must be in Washington, away from the telephone and the reporters and ready to act when the news broke. I dreaded the publicity of a hotel. I was sensitive about asking to stay with friends who might conceivably be embarrassed to be caught harboring the wife of "the top Russian espionage agent in this country." The alternative seemed to be a sofa in the living room of my husband's parents who lived in a small Washington apartment and didn't really have room for me. But that day luck dropped from heaven, as it did so many times to lighten the darkness of those weeks. The mother of an old and good friend invited me to stay with her in her charming little house in Georgetown. She knew Owen wasn't a Communist. She didn't have a job to lose. She lived alone and no one need know I was there. It was perfect, and will always be remembered gratefully.

I unloaded all the books and magazines and files in Mr. Fortas's office, where I spent the day. He was seeing all sorts of people, and stories were rife. I learned some things about McCarthy which didn't surprise me. Drew Pearson, Stewart Alsop, I. F. Stone and others had from time to time printed unsavory items about his past. These included income tax evasion (he once failed to report $42,000), a move for his disbarment (on grounds of violating the state constitution and the code of ethics of the American Bar Association), granting two-day divorces to accommodate people who had contributed to his campaign, and the destruction of official records. But much worse than any of these was his successful crusade last year to save from execution SS men convicted of the killing of three hundred and fifty unarmed American prisoners of war and one hundred Belgian civilians. I could picture how McCarthy's disgraceful antics must look in Afghanistan. Eleanor Breed, in San Francisco, sent me a verse which she called "The Mysterious West":

> To send our men to foreign shore
> (Jessup and Owen Lattimore)
> And bring them home and call them spies
> Is odd in Oriental eyes.

Drew Pearson was interested in the Mongols at the Hopkins and Abe asked me to talk with him about them. For a year we had had a group of Mongols at the university working with Owen in his program of studies about Mongolia. The oldest of the group was a "Living Buddha," a very high dignitary of the Lama Buddhist Church, who had been a close friend of ours ever since 1931 when he had had to flee from the Communist government in Outer Mongolia. Two younger men, who are here with their families, had been very active in the anti-Communist Mongol nationalist movement, and both had held trusted positions in the anti-Communist National Government of China. They had all had to get out of China before the Communists took over, and since Owen had been their chief sponsor in this country and had spent much time and money in getting them established here, Mr. Pearson thought they were a living argument that Owen could not be a Communist.

That day the most lurid story was one that all the newspapermen were talking about. McCarthy had told someone that the "Lattimore case" was another Hiss case, and that Owen's Whittaker Chambers was Joe Barnes — that Joe had been a Communist and to prove his repentance had joined the ranks of the ex-Communist informers and was going to tell all about his old friend Lattimore. We heard afterward that this bit of fantasy grew from McCarthy's telling a newspaperman, cryptically, that he had had a long talk with Joe. When McCarthy was later asked if the story was true he said he wished it were.

I had enlisted several friends to read Owen's books, looking for short quotations which would represent his real point of view without making people read through whole books or chapters. This was a difficult job for two reasons. First, everything he had ever written was written on the basic assumption that he was a loyal American who had the interests of his country at heart and that he opposed the spread of Communism anywhere in the world. He expected his readers to take this for granted and therefore had not thought it necessary constantly to repeat it, as Russian writers constantly have to repeat their rigmarole of devotion to Stalin and opposition to "western imperialism" in everything they write. The second difficulty was his scholarly approach. To a scholar nothing is ever simple or dogmatic enough to be said in one sentence. There are always qualifications, ifs, buts, and on the other hands. To represent his point of view fairly it was almost necessary to read a whole book, or at least a complete chapter. Taking sentences out of context could very easily distort his meaning completely, as we were to learn in detail later from McCarthy's staff workers.

Most of the excerpts from his writings which I, and the others, collected were too long. Nobody would bother to read them. We did find some short ones, however, which we felt expressed his point of view, in or out of context, such, for instance, as the following:

"[A safe American policy] would guarantee that the Chinese Communists remain in a secondary position, because it would strengthen those Chinese who are opposed to Communism. . . ." (Article in *Virginia Quarterly Review*, 1940.)

"Our cardinal need there is a united China, carried forward on a current of orderly reforms. There is no need for violent revolution; but, unless the current of orderly reforms is given a free channel, there will be violent revolution. It would be a tragic folly, and the culminating folly of two decades, if American vacillation and failure to support the patriots in China — the hard-pressed guardians of the American stake in evolutionary democratic progress —

should let loose defeatism, civil war and revolution. America has no time to lose. We must have a policy that does not limit us to defending the possessions of the democracies, but pledges us to support and spread democracy itself." (Article in magazine *Asia*, April 1941. Page 162.)

"I do not believe that a spread of Communism anywhere in Asia (or indeed in Europe or America) is either inevitable or desirable. . . . More than that, I believe that the country which most people in Asia would like to imitate and emulate is America rather than Russia." (Article in *China Monthly*, December 1945.)

"No Chinese Government can be genuinely independent if it is subject to manipulation by Russia." (Statement signed by Owen Lattimore together with Senator Flanders, Senator Murray, and Professors Dulles, Fisher and Mac-Nair, December 30, 1946.)

"Those of us who have never been Marxists have many straightforward disagreements with the Marxists." (Book review in the *New York Herald Tribune*, November 30, 1947.)

"The fact is that the American interest, of course and without further discussion, lies in making sure of the minimum expansion of Russian control and influence." (Lecture, Mt. Holyoke College, June 1948.)

"The spread of direct Russian control over Asia would be disastrous for the countries of Asia as well as for America and Europe." (*The Situation in Asia*, 1949. Page 12.)

"We shall have turned the disadvantage of an Asia that we are not strong enough to control into the advantage of an Asia strong enough to refuse to be controlled by Russia. We shall have given a fresh impetus to both capitalism and political democracy." (*The Situation in Asia*, 1949. Page 237.)

"At the same time, any new departure in United States policy in Asia must be proof against the accusation of 'appeasing' Communism as a doctrine or Russia as a state." (Article in the *Atlantic Monthly*, January 1950.)

Mr. Fortas had a "fact sheet" mimeographed including these and other quotations, a complete list of Owen's books and magazine articles (almost a hundred items), a brief sketch of his life, the dozen organizations to which he does belong (none of them subversive), and his actual relations with Russia, including one brief visit to Moscow on his way home from China but consisting chiefly of ignored requests for visas.

Abe Fortas suggested that I come to his house Sunday evening to listen to Drew Pearson talk about the Mongols. A lot of people were talking in the living room. We went upstairs and he put a tiny radio on the floor near where we were sitting. He knew what I didn't know, that Drew Pearson was going to state definitely that Owen was McCarthy's No. 1 spy, and that he was going to do it well. This is what he said:

WASHINGTON — I am now going to reveal the name of the man whom Senator McCarthy has designated the top Communist agent in the United States. Senator McCarthy has said that he would rest his entire charge of State Department Communism on this case. The man is Owen Lattimore of Johns Hopkins University. Dr. Lattimore is America's number one expert on China and the Far East, and, as such, served as adviser to Generalissimo Chiang Kai-shek, and later as adviser to General Marshall. He has not been with the State Department for five years, but he has continued his close contacts with the Orient. And here is the inside story of what he has been doing. When the Living Buddha of Mongolia was expelled by the Soviets, Owen Lattimore brought him to this country and helped support him, so that some day he could go back and fight against Communism. The Living Buddha is the spiritual leader for part of the Far East, and he has the same relation to Buddhists as the Pope to the Catholic world, so the Communists, who oppose all religion, put a price on his head. The Dalai Lami of Tibet first offered him a refuge, but Owen Lattimore, now accused of being a Communist, persuaded him to come to Baltimore, where he now lives. At the proper time, his influence in re-winning the Far East would be most important. Lattimore also brought two Mongolian Princes to Baltimore, each with a Soviet price on his head, and they have been living near the Lattimores, getting daily encouragement for the time when they may go back to the Far East; and oust the Communists. Today there was supposed to be a birthday party at the Lattimore home for a young Mongolian Prince, born in this country, named Owen — Owen Hangin, in honor of the American benefactor who helped his father. But thanks to all the furore in Washington, the party was called off. Senator McCarthy has claimed that three Communist agents came to this country to confer with Lattimore. But what McCarthy either did not know or concealed was that those agents were two Mongol Princes and the Living Buddha, fleeing from Communism, with a Soviet price on their heads.

NEW DELHI, INDIA — Owen Lattimore is now in Kabul, Afghanistan, sent by the Secretary General of the United Nations on an economic mission to bolster Afghanistan and keep it out of the hands of Russia. On the border between India and Russia, Afghanistan is one of the most important countries in the world in blocking the sweep of Communism into India. Meanwhile, Mrs. Lattimore and Detlev Bronk, President of Johns Hopkins, have asked for a Senate hearing. But no opportunity has been given to defend his name. Now I happen to know Owen Lattimore personally, and I only wish this country had more patriots like him.

There were inaccuracies in this broadcast, such as calling Owen an advisor of General Marshall, but the big thing was Drew Pearson's uncompromising recognition of Owen's patriotism. I could have hugged him.

At that very moment in Baltimore our Mongols *were* having a birthday party. It was to have been at our house and I felt sad to miss it. A few of them went to a neighbor's at six o'clock and came back to the party with a recording of Pearson's broadcast. They were delighted with it in spite of its many inaccuracies. Peter and John laughingly told their children that in America they had become princes and princesses. Dilowa Hutukhtu, the Living Buddha, had been made into a pope instead of just a high cardinal. But the important things were true, and they weren't accustomed to Americans knowing much about Mongols anyway.

So now Owen would be in all the headlines the next morning, and we could begin to fight in the open. By taking two pills I got some sleep that night. I had had very little in the past two weeks and had become too groggy to be useful.

That Monday morning, March 27, Abe Fortas really went into high gear. Some of the Page School boys came over, and we all pitched in to help prepare his ammunition. My morale soared with the arrival of Owen's first message from Afghanistan, the wonderful A.P. dispatch about

the charges being "pure moonshine" and McCarthy falling flat on his face.

Because of the interest Drew Pearson had aroused in the
Mongols Mr. Nikoloric, one of the younger members of
the law firm, was sent over to Baltimore to arrange a press
interview with them in Owen's office. He described to us
how Dilowa Hutukhtu, the Living Buddha, had sat in state
behind Owen's big desk in a dark red robe and scarlet and
gold brocaded vest, the two young men, Peter and John,
sitting beside him. Dilowa told the newspaper men about
how he had known Owen ever since he himself had first
fled from the Communists in 1931 and knew he was not pro-
Communist, and the young men said they knew that Owen
had had no connection with Mongol Communists but only
with the anti-Communist Mongol nationalist movement.
They all three told about their connections with the Kuomintang Government of China. Because McCarthy had suggested that they themselves might be pro-Communist they
knew they must also tell something about their own anti-
Communist connections and activities; but these they had
been cautious about talking about ever since the Communist
occupation of Inner Mongolia for fear of Communist re-
prisals against members of their families who are still there.
Loyalty to Owen made them run this risk, however, and
they told the newsmen that Peter had been a bodyguard
and John a secretary of Owen's old friend Prince Teh, who
is still holding out, with an army of five to ten thousand,
against Communist domination in western Mongolia.

Hundreds of indignant letters had been pouring in, from
friends and casual acquaintances and perfect strangers, and
a good many people who had written letters to Senator

Tydings and other congressmen had sent carbon copies to me or to the law firm. While we didn't want to quote from letters from friends without asking permission, and there was no time for that, the letters to senators seemed public property. A great many of the letters to senators were from people who knew Owen's work, either through his books or through professional associations of one kind or another, who were well qualified to speak of his standing as a scholar, his ideas and his character. Mr. Fortas asked the Page School boys to pick out quotations from them to give to the investigating committee.

That afternoon our sophomore son David arrived from Harvard. He had been working round the clock to get enough ahead on his studies so that he could come down to help me, and somehow I hadn't realized how lonely I had been until I saw him. We sat up late that night talking over everything that had happened, and Tuesday and Wednesday he worked with us at the office.

On Monday, the twenty-seventh, J. Edgar Hoover had appeared before the Tydings Committee to explain why it was impossible for the F.B.I. to open its files for their inspection. He told them that the mere fact that the F.B.I. had not forwarded a case of suspected disloyalty for prosecution could be taken to mean that there was no conclusive case, thereby implying that if the F.B.I. had evidence of espionage activities by Owen it would have acted against him long since. Senator Hickenlooper had then read a note from McCarthy asking Hoover to have an F.B.I. agent present when he addressed the Senate so that he could turn over to him documents which he claimed would prove that Owen was a Communist Party member and a Russian agent. This was a diabolical move on his part, because once the documents were in the hands of the F.B.I. they became secret. No one could know what, if anything, they proved, and McCarthy's description of them would be widely accepted. This would enable him to be even more atrociously irresponsible in his charges than he was the first time, and with more deadly effect.

When Abe heard about this dodge he sent McCarthy a telegram demanding that all documents be made public and warning him that the "hocus-pocus of attempting to create an air of mystery by referring to documents which you will dramatically turn over to the F.B.I. and will not make available for public appraisal" would be considered "obvious and apparent chicanery in which we are entitled to assume a United States senator will not indulge." When this telegram was released to the press on the morning of McCarthy's speech it at least warned the newspapermen of a new booby trap.

McCarthy had announced his speech for Tuesday, the 28th, but Abe hoped it could be put off until nearer the time of Owen's return, and was pleased when he heard it reported that Senator Paul Douglas, who was presiding over an extended senate debate on natural gas, had said that for the next two or three days he would refuse to recognize the Angel Gabriel unless he were going to talk about gas. Thursday afternoon McCarthy, substituting poison gas for natural gas, succeeded in making his speech.

David and I had come back to Ruxton late Wednesday evening. After Drew Pearson's broadcast both Owen's office and our house had been besieged by newspapermen. There seemed no point, however, in my saying anything at all at this point, so all calls had been referred to Abe Fortas who had borne the brunt of saying "no comment" for me, and saved me from an enormous amount of embarrassment. Abe's telephone rang constantly and people swarmed into his office, not only the press but all sorts of people who came with offers of help and advice. And when he went home after a long day they telephoned or came to his house. I dreaded to leave his protection to go home, but he was going up to New York and would be there Friday morning to meet Owen on his arrival. When we got home the telephone was still ringing, but David protected me by handling all the calls.

Thursday afternoon some of the Page School students went down to Associated Press headquarters to watch the teletype reports of McCarthy's speech as it was being made. The speech lasted for more than four hours and they telephoned me from time to time, but long before it was over they were thrown out because someone saw them taking notes.

We took the B. and O. night train up to New York to meet Owen. We had made our Pullman reservations in the name of "Mrs. Owens," just in case the ticket seller had a newspaper friend who might be on hand for an interview when we got to the station. But the ticket seller recognized us and was very friendly and solicitous. We bought all the evening papers, and went to bed as soon as the Pullman car was opened, so as to be as fresh as possible in the morning.

At seven-thirty in the morning, in New York, we telephoned Abe. He had thought the plane might be in early, but had just received the bad news that instead it had been delayed in Ireland and would not arrive until the following morning. He suggested that we have some breakfast and turn up at his hotel at nine o'clock.

We had breakfast with the Edward C. Carters. Mr. Carter had been Secretary General of the Institute of Pacific Relations when Owen had edited *Pacific Affairs*, and I wanted to see him because McCarthy's speech had dealt at length with the I.P.R. and Owen's connections with it, all still based on Kohlberg and the China Lobby, and had laid great stress on Owen's one visit to Moscow, where he had spent ten days with Mr. Carter on I.P.R. business in 1936. The present Secretary General, William Holland, and his family, also old friends of ours, were staying with the Carters and it made me happy to know I had the warm support and help of all of them. Mr. Carter gave me copies of old reports he and Owen had made to the I.P.R. about the Moscow visit and also a copy of a statement about it he had released to the press the night before. Mrs. Carter borrowed an apartment where we could spend the night, and later Bill Holland went over to see Mr. Fortas. 14459

We were distressed to find Abe Fortas suffering from a miserable cold, though it wasn't surprising, since he had been working under terrible strain for a week. He was rather frantic about Owen's delay in Shannon, as he thought it vital to issue some sort of a reply to McCarthy just as soon as possible. He called Owen on the trans-Atlantic telephone and we all spoke to him briefly. It was wonderful to hear his confident voice. Abe told him he would work on ideas for a press statement and would call him again just before twelve o'clock, when his plane was due to leave. He had a transcript of McCarthy's endless speech, and spent the next two hours picking out the points which he thought

Owen should reply to immediately. Then he waited for the call he had placed to come through. It was getting perilously near to twelve o'clock, and every few minutes he sent David to call the overseas operator. The lines to Shannon were busy. We were all feeling tense and jittery when twelve o'clock came and the call had not come. Dave tried the operator again. She reported that the plane was already on the runway. It seemed like an important defeat at the time, though as it turned out it probably didn't make a great deal of difference.

Paul Porter turned up at noon and went over the plans Abe had made for the press release, which now had to wait till the morrow. After lunch I read over the transcript of McCarthy's speech. It painted a picture of Owen so completely divorced from reality that it still seemed as if he must be talking about someone else — someone I had never met or heard of. I still couldn't believe that this could happen in the United States of America, and particularly that it could happen to us. Owen's voice over the telephone had sounded real, but nothing else seemed real at all. And the least real thing I had ever read was the transcript of McCarthy's speech.

Perhaps the most menacing part of his long tirade was his claim that he had a witness, trusted by the Department of Justice, who would testify that Owen "was known to him to be a member of the Communist Party, a member over whom they had disciplinary powers." The afternoon papers claimed that this witness was Louis Budenz, an ex-Communist who had turned Catholic and was a professor at Fordham University. When Abe heard this rumor he asked me his second, and last, question about Owen, and that indirectly. "Look here," he said, "I don't want to find that when Owen was a boy in his teens he foolishly joined something that turned out afterward to be Communist." I laughed. "You don't need to worry on that score," I said. "When Owen was in his teens he was the most unpolitical person you can imagine. When I first knew him he was interested in trade and travel and hunting and riding, and he really took very little interest in anything political until the Japanese invasion of China in 1937. And even after that he was woefully ignorant of Communism."

I spent part of the afternoon trying to get in touch with people in various parts of the country who could supply information which Owen would need in refuting some of McCarthy's charges. Before we needed this material every one of them had responded with wonderful letters.

Our borrowed apartment was beautiful, and gay with spring flowers sent by David's friend Emily. We dined with the Carters and the Hollands and went to bed early because Owen's plane was due to arrive at four in the morning. Abe telephoned at three to waken us, and before four was at our door in a United Nations car to take us to the airport. I had bravely urged him not to come because of his bad cold, but I knew we were in for an ordeal and was comforted to see him.

At Idlewild a large night crew of newsmen and photographers were drinking coffee and joking with each other while they waited for their prey. I normally like newspapermen, but now I dreaded them. My mind seemed numb and my heart leaden. How different this was from all Owen's other homecomings. Instead of the old private joy of seeing each other after his being far away there would be the public horror of greeting each other in front of massed cameras and the glare of newsreel lights, and the brazen questions about our private affairs. The wait seemed endless, but when Owen came at last into the crowded little waiting room the first sight of him lifted a weight from my heart and I knew that I was terribly glad he was home.

CHAPTER III

HERE Eleanor and I found that the dislocation of our lives began to spread out and affect the lives of other people. It was obvious that we were going to have to stay in Washington as long as it was necessary to carry on our fight. We did not want to stay in a hotel, because of the publicity, the telephone ringing all the time, and the newspapers wanting interviews or statements. We decided we would have to ask my parents to help us out. They are seventy-eight years old, and they live in a tiny apartment in Washington, the city in which they grew up, and in which two of their children are living. It would not be easy for my mother to move out, even for a few days, because she is under constant medical attention and was at that time getting ready for a serious eye operation. But she and my father did not hesitate for a minute at my suggestion that they move over to our Baltimore home and let us make their apartment our headquarters. Accordingly, early on Monday morning, April 3, we drove over to Washington. I did not have time even to see my parents. David took Eleanor and me to the lawyers' office and then went on to drive my parents back to Baltimore. We held a sort of council of war with Thurman Arnold, Abe Fortas, and Paul Porter, and then went over to the apartment, where

I set to work preparing my statement for the Senate Subcommittee.

David got back from Baltimore late that afternoon, and for the next few days he and Emily Lewis did all the marketing and cooking, and also carried messages all over Washington. The same afternoon Joe Barnes got to Washington. He had broken off a lecture tour in the South in order to come and help. Joe made himself an indispensable part of the team. He is one of my oldest and closest friends. As a foreign correspondent for years with an expert knowledge both of Western Europe and Soviet Russia, as a correspondent who has also several times visited the Far East, as former Foreign Editor of the *New York Herald Tribune* and editor of the *New York Star*, he is one of the top newspapermen in America.

Joe announced right away that his job was going to be to make himself unpleasant. Throughout the discussion of strategy and tactics and the drafting of statements, he was going to "toughen me up." He was going to think and talk as if he were a hostile reporter, probing for weak points or gaps in my statement, thinking up mean or "angled" questions, and generally badgering me as if I were a suspicious character. He did a wonderful job.

Monday began frantically, because my hearing had originally been set for the next day, Tuesday. However, Senator Tydings, in view of the delay in my return from Afghanistan, very considerately deferred the hearing until Thursday, so we had a little more time in which to work. As soon as I knew that, I telephoned to Stanley Salmen, executive vice-president of Little, Brown and Company, my publishers. He flew down that afternoon from Boston. He had worked closely with me on my three previous books and I have a profound respect for his editorial gift of orderly arrangement and presentation. So with me drafting, Joe as rewrite man and tough guy, Stanley as editor and Abe Fortas as general and legal advisor, we now had a team.

The Johns Hopkins group who had helped Eleanor came over to Washington every day to prepare material to document our refutation of the almost one hundred misstatements of fact which were contained in McCarthy's speech of March 30. They also made a striking analysis of the misquotations and the quotations taken out of context which McCarthy had used to distort the meaning of my writings.

The fighting spirit and fast accurate research of this Hopkins team, headed by George Kahin and including Dave Wilson, Martin Ring and Dick Schraml, with help from John De Francis, Ruth Bean and Natalie Gurney, was a demonstration of loyalty that any university professor in America would envy.

My secretary, Margie McKim, shuttled back and forth between Baltimore and Washington. I do not yet know how it was possible for her to put in so much time in Washington and still keep my office in Baltimore going. At the Page School, Bill Austin, John De Francis, Harold Vreeland, and our three Mongols, the Dilowa Hutukhtu, John Hangin, and Peter Onon, kept things going so well that in spite of all the disruption, only one lecture was missed during the whole period.

Between our drafting team at my parent's apartment, the research team, the legal office, my university office, and my parents, with whom she kept in touch by telephone,

Eleanor acted as chief of staff. Herbert Elliston, editor of the *Washington Post*, said later on: "It's a lucky thing for Owen Lattimore that he didn't marry an ordinary wife." I am, I suppose, like a typical professor in my way of working. I assemble a mass of material, and then work inward from the edges of it toward the center. Eleanor has the right kind of mind for a chief of staff. Mentally, she is always able to put herself right at the center of things. In addition to everything else she was to a large extent the one who dealt with the press and with the friends and strangers who were sending advice, supporting letters, and very often material and ammunition of priceless value to us from all over the country. And, at the expense of her own strength, she babied me, always thinking of my food, my clothes, and driving me to bed early to make sure that I got enough sleep. By the time that I got back from Afghanistan, she had been driving herself so hard, getting so little sleep, and living so much just on her nerve that she had already lost twelve pounds.

A couple of days later we got a telegram from some old friends of ours, telling us that they were out West and asking us to make use of their house as long as we were in Washington. This eased things a great deal. We moved over to their house and David drove to Baltimore and brought my parents back to their apartment. I still had not had time to see them.

I do not know how many hours a day we worked, but by Wednesday afternoon, several hours after the deadline set by Abe Fortas, we had the forty-two-page statement drafted and documented. Abe then did the final work on it, and went over it with his partners, and by doing an all-night overtime mimeographing job it was ready for distribution to the press early next morning.

On Thursday, when I woke up, I found I was relaxed and not nervous. Eleanor and Abe and Joe and the others had all been satisfied with the statement. There was going to be nothing to worry about there. The big problem was that of facing a totally new kind of experience. I had never even seen a Senatorial Committee in action, as a spectator, and now I was going to have to face one, plus a crowd that might be either hostile or friendly, but would certainly be hungry for sensation.

We drove down to the office and went on from there with Abe Fortas and Paul Porter. When we came into the Caucus Room it was already crowded, with people standing all around the walls. I was surprised at how quickly, in the sea of strange people, I saw faces that I knew. There were my father and mother, whom I had not seen for more than a month. They looked white and frail and tired. There were all the Page School crowd, including our three Mongols, and a few others from the university. Here and there I recognized Washington friends. It made me feel better.

There was some pushing around before we could get seated. Photographers wanted pictures of Eleanor and me. The klieg lights went on for the newsreel and television cameras. They were mostly right in my face, and greatly increased the eye strain in reading my statement. A little knot of cameramen squatted on the floor, in front of me and to the left. Most of them wanted to get pictures of me during the hearing, showing animation or emotion or an arresting gesture. All day, their flash bulbs kept going off at unpredictable intervals, adding to the strain.

I sat at a little table, with Abe Fortas on my right. Eleanor sat just behind with Paul Porter on her right. We faced the long table at which sat the senators, representatives of the investigative staff of the Subcommittee, and several visiting senators. From their photographs, I quickly recognized Senator Millard E. Tydings, Democrat, of Maryland, Chairman of the Subcommittee, with Green of Rhode Island and McMahon of Connecticut, Democrats, on his left and Hickenlooper of Iowa and Lodge of Massachusetts, Republicans, on his right. At the same table I recognized Senator Tom Connally of Texas and back of this table there were not only newsreel and television cameras but several rows of spectators. From his photographs, I quickly recognized McCarthy. He was sitting back and slightly to one side of Senator Tydings, so that when I was looking toward the chairman I could look squarely at him too. I soon found out something interesting. Joe McCarthy cannot look you straight in the eye.

Senator Tydings called me to be sworn in. I stood up, he administered the oath, and I sat down to read my statement, leading off with a direct attack on McCarthy, in order to make it clear right at the beginning that the charges against my loyalty were not only false charges but charges made by a man so irresponsible in his conduct and so little deserving belief that he was in fact not worthy of the office of United States Senator.

I wish to express to you my appreciation for this opportunity to reply to the statements about me which have been made by Senator Joseph McCarthy of Wisconsin. The Senator has in effect accused me of disloyalty and treason. He made these accusations when I was in Afghanistan, and I did not hear of them until some days after they were first made.

The technique used by the Senator in making these charges is apparently typical. He first announced at a press conference that he had discovered "the top Russian espionage agent in the United States." At this time he withheld my name. But later, after the drama of his announcement was intensified by delay, he whispered my name to a group of newspapermen, with full knowledge that it would be bandied about by rumor and gossip and eventually published. I say to you that this was unworthy of a Senator or an American.

As I shall show in detail, McCarthy's charges are untrue. As soon as I heard of the substance of the charges I denounced them for what they were: base and contemptible lies. In fact, as I recall, on several occasions I used somewhat more colorful words.

Gentlemen, I want you to know that it is most distasteful to me to use language concerning a United States Senator which, to say the least, is disrespectful. To me, the honor and responsibility of American citizenship carry with them an obligation to respect the high office of a member of the United States Senate. But that office, the position of United States Senator, likewise carries with it a responsibility which this man Joseph McCarthy has flagrantly violated. As a citizen who holds no official position, it is my right and duty to list these violations which are illustrated by the Senator's conduct in my own case.

He has violated it by impairing the effectiveness of the United States Government in its relations with its friends and allies, and by making the Government of the United States an object of suspicion in the eyes of the anti-Communist world, and undoubtedly the laughing stock of the Communist governments.

He has violated it by instituting a reign of terror among officials and employees in the United States Government, no one of whom can be sure of safety from attack by the machine gun of irresponsible publicity in Joseph McCarthy's hands.

He has without authorization used secret documents obtained from official government files.

He has vilified citizens of the United States and accused them of high crime, without giving them an opportunity to defend themselves.

He has refused to submit alleged documentary evidence to a duly constituted committee of the Senate.

He has invited disrespect to himself and his high office by refusing to live up to his word. Twice on the floor of the Senate he stated that any charges that he made under the cloak of immunity, he would repeat in another place so that their falseness could be tested in a court of the United States. He said that if he should fail to do this he would resign. He has been called to repeat his charges so that they could be tested in a court action. He has failed to do so. And he has not resigned.

Gentlemen, I speak to you as a private citizen. I owe no obligation to anyone except my country and my conscience. I have spent my life in the study of the problems of the Far East, and, as an author and journalist, in writing about those problems as I saw them. I have written eleven books, and literally hundreds of newspaper and magazine articles. Too few people in this country have realized the importance of the Far East — of China, Mongolia, Tibet, India, Pakistan, Afghanistan. These areas of the world seem to most Americans to be merely places in a travel book. I have been trying all my life to arouse interest in this area and to spread knowledge of it in this country.

Now, suddenly, this nation is beginning to awaken to the

fact that the Far East may be a center of the political crisis in which we find ourselves. That is a hopeful development. From this awakening, public debate is bound to result; and through public debate, the nation should be able to evolve policies toward China and the Far East which we will carry out in the same spirit of patriotic nonpartisanship which has, until recently, distinguished our conduct of foreign affairs in Europe.

But before this essential public debate on China policy can take place, there are some things that have to be cleared away.

First, it is possible for people, including officials of the United States Government, to oppose further aid to the Nationalist Government of China without being disloyal to the United States, or pro-Communist.

Second, persons, including officials, who opposed further aid to the Nationalist Government — or who advocated a reduction of that aid, after the end of the war with Japan — were not necessarily disloyal to the United States or pro-Communist.

Third, citizens of the United States, including State Department officials engaged on Far Eastern work, are presumptively loyal and devoted to their country.

Fourth, persons who are engaging in violent propaganda for all-out aid to the Nationalist Government in Formosa and to Generalissimo Chiang Kai-shek, do not have a monopoly of opposition to Communism. Some of these people are undoubtedly sincere; but none of them is entitled to assert his views by vilification and personal abuse of others, or by unfounded attacks upon officials of the United States Government.

Now it is obvious that Senator McCarthy and I differ on each of these points. Judging from his unquestioning acceptance and extensive use of the propaganda of the so-called China Lobby, he is at least its willing tool. The Senator seems to feel that everyone is disloyal whose opinions do not agree with those of himself and the China Lobby with respect to total and complete commitment of the United States to the Nationalist Government of China. Some of his denunciations are understandable only on the theory that he believes that anyone is disloyal whose opinions on China policy during the last nine or ten years parallel or support those of the Government of the United States. In the latter category the Senator would have to include General George C. Marshall, General Stilwell, and presumably the various Secretaries of State, Messrs. Hull, Stettinius, Byrnes and Acheson.

In fact, I wonder a bit how a man so young as Joseph McCarthy, whose acquaintance with national and international affairs is so recent, can have become such a great expert on the difficult and complex problem of China and the Far East. My wonder on this score increased when I read his speech on the Senate floor. Some of his material is from Chinese and Russian sources. Or perhaps I should say that some of his exotic material on Mongolia appears to trace back to some Russian source of distinctly low caliber.

I did not know that the Senator was a linguist. But really, the material that the Senator read is so badly translated and so inaccurate that I am sure that I should not like to place the blame for it on the learned Senator. Indeed, I fear that the sound and fury come from the lips of McCarthy, but that there is an Edgar Bergen in the woodpile. And I fear that *this* Edgar Bergen is neither kindly nor disinterested.

In any event, the Senator has stated that he will stand or fall on my case. I hope this will turn out to be true, because I shall show that his charges against me are so empty and baseless that the Senator will fall, and fall flat on his face. I trust that the Senator's promise that he will retire from the arena if his charges against me fail is not as insincere as his twice-repeated promise to resign if he should fail to repeat his libelous accusations in a forum which would expose him to suit. I hope the

Senator will in fact lay his machine gun down. He is too reckless, careless and irresponsible to have a license to use it.

It is somewhat difficult to pin down the Senator's accusations against me. He first mentioned me on March 13 in a statement before this Subcommittee. At that time, according to
Senator McCarthy, I was merely a humble fellow who was
just "pro-Communist." On March 21 McCarthy told a press
conference that an unnamed man connected with the State Department was — I quote — "the top Russian espionage agent in
the United States." Subsequently, McCarthy identified me as
this top espionage agent in a meeting attended by various
persons.

It is significant to note that my eminent position as "the top
espionage agent" was apparently an afterthought. When
McCarthy first made his sensational charges on February 20 in
which he said that there are 57 Communists in the State Department and 205 bad security risks — not one of which he has
produced, he apparently did not have me in mind, directly or
indirectly, referring to three other cases as "the big three."

My eminence therefore, as the top Russian espionage agent
dawned upon the Senator rather late in his crusade. It didn't
last very long. I was pretty quickly demoted from the position
of big fish to relatively small fry.

In his major broadside on the Senate floor on March 30, the
Senator, quite understandably, showed that he was getting a
bad case of weak knees. In that speech the worst charge that
he made against me was that I was "*one* of the top Communist agents in this country." You will note that I was merely
one among many; and that I was no longer guilty of espionage.
Indeed, he suggested that maybe the best way to describe me
was as a "bad policy risk"; and the poor fellow ended up on
page 4446 of the *Record* by saying that "I fear in the case of
Lattimore, I may have perhaps placed too much stress on the

question of whether or not he has been an espionage agent"!

Now I can understand why the Senator wants to weasel, particularly in view of his brave — but I fear insincere — statements that he would stand or fall on my case and that he would repeat his statements in an unprivileged forum or would resign. But I think that I would be the instrument of a great service to the country if the Senator should resign, and I want to deal with each of his charges.

At the outset, however, I should like to make clear just what my connections with the State Department and the United States Government have been. The fact is that I have and have had no connection with the Department and the Department does not consult me and has not consulted me, except as follows:

(1) I was appointed by the President as a member of the Pauley Reparations Mission to Japan and served in this capacity for three or four months, beginning October 15, 1945. Although this was a White House mission, I was paid by the State Department for my services.

(2) I participated in a two-day panel discussion of China problems at the State Department in October of 1949. The members of this panel included about 25 or 30 specialists from universities, business, and public life. Among them were General George C. Marshall, Harold Stassen, and John D. Rockefeller, III. It was while this conference was in preparation that I wrote a memorandum, at the specific request of the State Department, giving my views on China policy.

(3) On June 5, 1946 I lectured on Japanese problems at the State Department. It is my understanding that this was one of a series of lectures to State Department personnel presented by persons of various points of view.

Other than this, I have never been a consultant for the State Department or on its payroll. I do not have a desk in the State Department. I do not have a telephone there. I do not have — and never have had — access to State Department files. The Senator must know that these statements of his are untrue.

My only other employment record with the federal government is that during the War, from 1942 to 1945, I was first Deputy Director of Pacific Operations, and then a Consultant, for the Office of War Information.

In July, 1941, I was appointed as Political Adviser to Generalissimo Chiang Kai-shek. I was appointed by the Generalissimo upon recommendation of President Roosevelt. At the end of the six months' period for which I was appointed, the Generalissimo urged me to accept reappointment for one year. In February, 1942, I returned to the United States, then went back to Chungking, and about the end of 1942 offered my resignation. The Generalissimo graciously refused to accept my resignation formally, but asked me to consider myself on indefinite leave.

One of Senator McCarthy's astonishing affidavits alleged that I was sent back to the United States because the Generalissimo was displeased with me. I therefore entered in the record at this point the following letter from him to President Roosevelt in 1942:

HEADQUARTERS OF THE GENERALISSIMO
CHINA

Chungking, Szechuan
12 January 1942

DEAR MR. PRESIDENT:
I am happy to have the opportunity afforded by Mr. Lattimore's return to America on a short visit, to send

you a word of greeting, and to thank you for recommending him as my political adviser.

Mr. Lattimore has fully measured up to our expectations and has entirely justified your choice. You unerringly detected the right man to select to act as a counsellor at a time when decisions which will affect the whole world for generations to come are in the balance. He has not only a wide knowledge of our language, history and geography, he has in addition an invaluable understanding of our contemporary political affairs. His absolute integrity is manifest in everything that he does or says, and I never have the slightest doubt that any suggestion that he may make is based upon a genuine desire to assist China to the utmost of his power.

The various Missions that you have sent to China are doing valuable work. They and the visits of various members of your Government have greatly helped to bring America closer to us. Personal contacts necessarily tend to promote closer and more understanding relationship and friendship. You may be assured that all the American Missions are going about their duties with a zeal that promises permanently useful results.

Since the Japanese attacks on Pearl Harbor, the Philippines and Hongkong, the Pacific problem has become more acute. It is fortunate that under your wise and steadfast leadership, the future outcome of our concerted struggle against treachery and barbarity is assured. I assure you that I shall do my utmost to help bring about a world order based upon justice tempered with mercy.

Mr. Lattimore will personally convey to you my views on some important matters upon which I have not touched above. If there are messages you wish to send me, I should appreciate you entrusting them to Mr. Lattimore to be conveyed to me upon his return to China.

Madame Chiang joins me in sending best wishes to you and Mrs. Roosevelt.

Yours sincerely,
CHIANG KAI-SHEK

President Franklin D. Roosevelt
The White House
Washington, D.C.

At this point I want to deal with Senator McCarthy's charge that I am the top Russian espionage agent in this country. As I have said, the Senator has backed away from this accusation and would probably prefer that it be forgotten. But I don't want it to be forgotten that the Senator made the charge. It is an accusation of a base crime, the crime of obtaining and supplying secret information to a foreign nation. In his entire four-hour speech, in which he has dredged up and slung at me all the mud that he could accumulate from all sources, however polluted, McCarthy does not recite a single act or circumstance which even on its face supports this vile accusation.

The nearest he comes to any attempt specifically to charge me with being a Soviet agent is to refer to a trip that I made to Point Barrow, Alaska, in May of 1949. He says that I had two cameras with me on that trip, and that I have a room in Baltimore devoted to "special photographic equipment."

I then took up this charge in detail. I had gone to Point Barrow as alternate for the president of the Johns Hopkins University, to attend a meeting of the Arctic Research Laboratory Advisory Board to discuss research work being done there by various universities under Navy grant. None of that work was "classified," and accordingly I was able to put a copy of the minutes of this meeting into the record.

McCarthy himself had said that everybody on the trip had carried two cameras. I, as a matter of fact, had carried only one. Since we were traveling under Navy facilities we all, of course, took pictures only when assured that it was permitted. I had all my Kodachrome slides with me, and there was considerable laughter at the mention of "Eskimo children, dog sleds, huts lined with whaleribs, natural beauties and sunsets." Incidentally, the "special photographic equipment" in my house is an ordinary dub photographer's darkroom in which my son and I develop our pictures when we have the time.

I then took up McCarthy's assertion that he had an affidavit from a former Red general who was supposed to have talked to another Red general in 1935 or 1936. The second Red general, according to the story, told the first Red general that they were getting good intelligence reports about Mongolia and the Far East through the Institute of Pacific Relations which, the second Red general said, the Soviet Intelligence had taken over through Communists in the United States. This yarn is best dealt with by inserting here a letter which Demaree Bess, Associate Editor of the *Saturday Evening Post* and in the 1930's *Christian Science Monitor* correspondent in the Far East and Moscow, wrote to Senator Tydings. Later he made a special trip to Washington to appear before the committee but he was not given time to do more than read this letter into the record.

Paris
April 7

Dear Senator Tydings:

I am writing to you because Owen Lattimore was my house guest during his visit to Moscow in 1936 about which Senator McCarthy has raised questions before your subcommittee. Mr. Lattimore stayed with me because he was — and is — an old and valued friend whom I had known intimately during my previous ten years in the Far East as correspondent for American newspapers.

There was nothing mysterious about Mr. Lattimore's visit to Moscow; he came there as the editor of *Pacific Affairs*, a publication of the Institute of Pacific Relations. As you probably know, the Institute was organized into national groups, and the Soviet group was then an active participant.

As I had already worked in Russia for more than two years, I was able to help Mr. Lattimore meet some Russians. In particular, I introduced him to a Soviet consular official I had met as a reporter, and who had spent some time in Mongolia, a country about which Mr. Lattimore was — and is — the foremost American specialist. This Soviet official (whose name I have forgotten) was very friendly and helpful to Mr. Lattimore — as he had been to me — and introduced him to other Russian experts on Mongolia and Central Asia and guided him through Moscow museums and libraries devoted to these subjects. At that period, the great purges had not yet started in Russia, and it was much easier for Americans to meet Russians than it later became.

Mr. Lattimore reported to me the results of his meetings with Russians. He was understandably impressed by the extent of Russian material concerning Russo-Chinese border regions — which seem very remote to Americans but are not so remote to Russians. Mr. Lattimore told me that, for the first time in his experience, he had met specialists who knew more than he did on this exotic subject.

In a speech on the Senate floor, Senator McCarthy mentioned an affidavit by an unnamed Russian who has reported a 1936 conversation with a Soviet intelligence officer who boasted that his organization was getting valuable information through the Institute of Pacific Relations, and especially through Mr. Lattimore. All that proves — in my opinion — is that the Soviet intelligence officers were as smart as I myself was at the time — because I, too, was getting valuable background material for my articles from the Institute's specialized reports and from conversations with Mr. Lattimore and other Americans workings for the Institute.

But perhaps the Soviet intelligence officer mentioned in Senator McCarthy's affidavit was not quite so smart as he thought, because there is no doubt in my mind that Mr. Lattimore learned considerably more from the Russians during that Moscow visit than they did from him — and this information has since been made available through Mr. Lattimore to our own intelligence services and to the State Department.

During my many years' friendship with Mr. Lattimore in China he never showed any special interest in Russia except insofar as the Russians were concerned with Mongolia and Central Asia, his chosen field of research and exploration. To my certain knowledge, Mr. Lattimore devoted almost his entire time during the 1936 Moscow visit to this same specialty. Those were the years when it was popular in the United States to be a "pink," but I never saw even the slightest evidence that Mr. Lattimore was becoming even the mildest form of "fellow traveler."

You may use this letter, in whole or in part, in any way you see fit. My own record is available in *Who's*

Who in America. I think that my articles in the *Saturday Evening Post* during the war — when it was not popular to be critical of Russia — are sufficient evidence of my own personal views about the Soviet system.

Sincerely yours,
DEMAREE BESS

McCarthy's "Red general" charge was an insinuation that the Institute of Pacific Relations was in 1936 a tool of Soviet Intelligence. The Institute of Pacific Relations is represented in a number of countries. The American Institute is a research and educational organization which a recent Rockefeller Foundation report called "the most important single source of independent studies of the problems of the Pacific Area and the Far East." Its present chairman is Gerard Swope, Honorary President of International General Electric. Among its trustees are General George Marshall, W. R. Herod of International General Electric, and C. K. Gamble, Director, Standard Vacuum Oil Company.

In 1945 Kohlberg, in his attack on the Institute which I have already described, was defeated in a proxy fight, receiving only sixty-six votes from the two thousand members of the Institute. At the time of this fight the Institute was defended by many of its distinguished members, trustees and officers, including Edwin Embree, Sumner Welles, W. W. Waymack, Arthur H. Dean, Robert Gordon Sproul and Ray Lyman Wilbur.

McCarthy's attack on the Institute, through his attacks on Ambassador Jessup and myself, was clearly a continuation of the old Kohlberg attack, as I was able to show by handing in for the record an eleven-page analysis, prepared by some of my students, showing in parallel columns the Kohlberg charges and the McCarthy charges. The identity of wording was so startling that it led to a number of newspaper articles on the activities of Kohlberg and the China Lobby.

My statement continued:

There is, however, one other insinuation specifically relating to me in connection with the Institute that I should like to answer. That is a statement to the effect that in 1936 I was in Moscow "obviously receiving instructions from the Soviet Government concerning the line which the Institute of Pacific Relations ought to follow." The Committee will remember that, according to one of Senator McCarthy's informants, in the year 1936, I was at least not *yet* a Communist!

Now the facts are these: In 1936 I was, as I have stated, resident in Peking, China, as editor of the Institute's magazine, *Pacific Affairs*. I was returning to the United States, and planned to stop off in various countries. E. C. Carter, Secretary General of the Institute, was in Moscow, where he was attempting — an attempt that in the long run proved fruitless — to persuade the Russians to take part in the research and discussions of the Institute of Pacific Relations with something that approached the give and take that prevailed among most of the national groups and which made the Institute a valuable and constructive international forum.

As editor of *Pacific Affairs*, I had published an article which included an uncomplimentary personal reference to Stalin. The Russians considered this a high crime and misdemeanor and were angry with me for publishing what they referred to as a Trotskyist version of events in China. At the same time, I had a particular reason for being displeased with them, be-

cause they had just published a review of one of my books
in which it was insinuated that I was a Japanese agent.

During the same visit I took part, by invitation, in a group
discussion of academic research workers on the social and
economic structure of China. One of Senator McCarthy's informants, Freda Utley, was present. Whatever her politics,
she was then clearly working for the Russians. The discussion
was hardly a success. The interpreting was bad. I could not
understand what the Russians were trying to say, and I did
not make myself popular when I quoted a book about China
by an ex-Communist.

I later delivered to the Soviet Academy of Sciences a lecture
on the Far East which I repeated in two cities in Holland and
again in London and which was then published in the journal
of the Royal Institute of International Affairs in London.

I also talked in Moscow with Ambassador William C. Bullitt
about why I thought my interpretation of the situation in
Inner Mongolia was right, and the Soviet interpretation wrong.
He exclaimed that the Soviet Foreign Office ought to know
that, and at his suggestion he then took me to see a Soviet
vice-commissar of Foreign Affairs, whose name I forget, to
whom I spoke my piece, in Ambassador Bullitt's presence and
at his request.

You may remember, gentlemen, that it was just about this
time that Mr. Roy Howard of Scripps-Howard and United
Press had recently been in Moscow, where he interviewed
Stalin. (Mr. Howard had also been interested in Mongolia. It
was in this interview that he got from Stalin a statement, sensational at the time, that if the Japanese attacked Mongolia
Russia would come to the aid of the Mongols.)

I then took up one of McCarthy's most absurd cloak-
and-dagger yarns — the charge that I had been a leader in

several pro-Russian student uprisings in China. This fantastic tale was dealt with summarily in the following letter from Nelson T. Johnson, former Ambassador to China.

DEAR LATTIMORE:

I have your letter of April 2 in regard to the charge that you were "a leader in several pro-Russian student uprisings in China." I was resident in Peking I think throughout the whole of the period between 1930 and 1937 and I recall your presence in Peking very clearly. At the moment, I do not remember how much of that period you were actually in Peking, but I know that you and your family had a home there for most of that time and that my wife and I enjoyed the hospitality of your home and that you were both frequently in our home. I recall very clearly that this period coincided with the invasion of Manchuria by Japan and I remember long conversations with you at various times about your work and the travels that you made into Mongolia and into Manchuria, for you were at that time working on the manuscript of a book which was to be published under the title of *Inner Asian Frontiers of China*. I was in a position at Peking in those days, being chief of the American diplomatic mission to China, where if there had been any report of complaint in regard to your activities among the Chinese of a political or seditious character, I would have been informed. I am sure that any information of that kind would have made an impression upon me and that I would not have forgotten it.

I am surprised to learn that you have been charged with having been a leader in several pro-Russian student uprisings in China during that period. I do not remember ever having heard of anything of that kind. I do not recall ever having heard that you were a participant in student troubles of any kind. On the contrary, it is my recollection that throughout this period your interests were in the research which you were living in Peking for the purpose of carrying out among the Mongols and the peoples of Manchuria, and that your work had nothing whatever to do with student movements.

With kindest personal regards, I am
Very truly yours,
NELSON T. JOHNSON

I also presented letters to the same effect from Colonel William Mayer who was then Military Attaché, United States Embassy in China, and from Dr. T. L. Yuan, who was then the Director of the Chinese National Library.

Next Senator McCarthy refers to a trip that I made with Philip J. Jaffe and T. A. Bisson in Yenan. I made such a trip, some time in 1937. I had known Bisson slightly as a Far Eastern student, when he was working for the Foreign Policy Association in New York City. I had never before met Jaffe, but I knew of him as the sponsor of a new magazine, *Amerasia*, of which I had become a board member. I also knew that he was a wealthy manufacturer of Christmas cards. He wanted to make a trip to Yenan, and he and Bisson wanted me to accompany them because of my knowledge of the area and the language. I was quite interested in going.

The Communists had taken over that area only about a year before. Several newspaper men had got in and every news-paperman in China was trying to get in. It was the biggest news story in China and all papers in Europe and America were eating it up. I had never had any contacts with any

Communists in China and I felt that this trip might enable me to round out my knowledge of the country.

Later I found and turned in to the Committee the notes I had made while in Yenan, showing the routine nature of our interviews. These notes would have enabled me to write articles like those of all the journalists who were trying to get the story of the Chinese Communists at that time; but I had written no articles as the Chinese Communists were not my specialty.

There is one additional matter in the McCarthy statement which might possibly be construed as an attempt to connect me with the improper procuring or sending of information to the Soviet Union. It is an attempt to connect me with the *Amerasia* case. You will recall that in 1945 some of the people connected with that magazine, as well as John S. Service [of the Department of State] and Andrew Roth [who at that time was in the Navy and later became a newspaper correspondent abroad] were arrested on charges relating to the unlawful procurement and possession of government documents. Service was not indicted, and the indictment against Roth was dropped.

I had been on the board of *Amerasia* from its founding in 1937 until 1941 when I resigned. I was never active as a board member. I consented to go on the board largely because I wanted to show that *Pacific Affairs*, the magazine of which I was editor, did not object to, but welcomed, other periodicals in the same field.

It will be noted that I had no connection with *Amerasia* after 1941, four years before the arrests in the case that Senator McCarthy mentions.

Nevertheless, the Senator attempts on the most flimsy and transparent basis to insinuate, without saying so, that I had some connection with the *Amerasia* arrests in 1945. He refers to an affidavit, which he has refused to supply, to the effect that the night before Service, Roth and four codefendants in the *Amerasia* case were arrested, both Service and Roth were at my house.

The person or persons who made the alleged statements to the Senator are reported by him to have stated that they were present at my house at the time; that Roth, Service and I "spent a great deal of time by themselves, discussing certain papers or manuscripts," and that our actions seemed strange at the time. One of these persons was reported to have said that I subsequently told him that the three of us "had been declassifying secret documents."

This is one of those fanciful distortions that has a remote but perverted relationship to fact. On the Sunday three days prior to the arrests in the *Amerasia* case, Mr. Service and Mr. Roth were at my house. I arranged a small picnic at which, as I recall, we ate hamburgers which I cooked on the open fire. There were present, in addition to Roth and Service, Professor Malcolm C. Moos of the John Hopkins University and his fiancée, and Professor George F. Carter of the Johns Hopkins University and his wife and children. Nothing whatever strange was going on. Roth had brought with him the galley proofs of his forthcoming book *Dilemma in Japan*, and asked me to read them. The material for this book had all been cleared by U. S. Navy security officers.

The papers or manuscript that the three of us were discussing, then, were nothing but the galley or script of a young author who wanted to get my opinion of his work. There were no government documents involved, nothing was classified or declassified, and there was absolutely nothing unusual about the entire matter. The allegation that I stated that we were declassifying secret documents is as absurd as it is untrue.

At this point I filed a memorandum from Professor Moos, giving his recollections of the day. Professor Carter, asked by my lawyers to make a statement, never replied.

I then took up McCarthy's attempt to prove my Red taint by connecting me with Henry Wallace.

In 1944 I was appointed to Mr. Wallace's mission to Siberia and China in my official capacity as representative of the Office of War Information. Throughout the mission, not being a member of the diplomatic service, I was quite properly excluded from high-level interviews and discussions, except on one occasion when I served as supplementary interpreter. I did not know about the existence of a "Wallace Report" until it was mentioned in the newspapers, and certainly was not consulted about it.

This wound up my rebuttal of the specific charges made by McCarthy; but I had still to deal with his threat that he would identify me with the Communist Party through a mysterious witness, rumored to be Louis Budenz. My statement therefore went on:

The Senator says that this alleged witness is trusted by the Department of Justice and has been used as a Government witness; that this witness has been a member of the Communist Party for a number of years; and that it is part of his work to distinguish between Party members and fellow travelers.

I do not know the name of this alleged witness. With full and complete realization of the serious implications and consequences of what I am to say; having in mind the advice of counsel that a member of the Communist Party may presumably decline, on constitutional grounds, to state whether he is or has been a member of the Communist Party; I make to you on my solemn oath the following statement:

I am not and never have been a member of the Communist Party. I have never been affiliated or associated with the Communist Party. I have never believed in the principles of Communism nor subscribed to nor advocated the Communist or Soviet form of government either within the United States, in China, in the Far East, or anywhere in the world. I have never consciously or deliberately advocated or participated in promoting the cause of Communism anywhere in the world.

For many years, the situation in the Far East has been such that no person could study its problems without undertaking to acquaint himself as thoroughly as possible with the facts about the Communist position and plans in the various countries of that area. I have made it my business, both as a scholar and as a journalist, to accumulate as much information on this as possible, and the results of my studies have all been published.

I have tried to avoid wishful thinking and self-delusion. I have tried, as emphatically as I could, to warn the people of this nation that the Communist threat in China and other countries of the Far East is very real indeed; that some of their appeals to the people of Asia are profound. I have tried to point out that it is our task, if we are to stem the advance of Communism, to make an appeal to the people of Asia which is not merely equal to that of the Communists, but so far greater that these people would have no doubt as to who are their true friends.

For the purpose of acquiring the information upon which I based my studies and conclusions, I talked and corresponded with informed people all over the world, without regard to whether they were Communists, anti-Communists, politicians or scholars. Since the middle 1930's, communications even with scholars in Communist countries have been more and more cut off. All the more for that reason, like any other student who is worth his salt in this field, I have eagerly seized upon every opportunity to obtain information through chinks and crevasses in the wall of fear and suppression that Communism builds around its informed people. For instance, while I was on the Pauley Reparations Mission to Japan in 1945 I made an effort to see some Japanese Communists because I thought their future activity in Japanese politics was going to be important, and succeeded in seeing Tokuda, one of their two top men. In 1947 I made an attempt to get to Outer Mongolia but was completely baffled. Way back in 1936, when I was about to return to China I even paid a call on Earl Browder, hoping I might open up a lead to information about the Chinese Communists; and during the war, of course, on the instructions of Chiang Kai-shek, I had several conversations with Chou En-lai. None of these contacts, or attempted contacts, however, provided me with access to permanent or reliable information from within the iron curtain in which each individual Communist wraps himself.

I then quoted criticisms of my books in Russian and American Communist publications, and continued:

As a matter of fact, gentlemen, I am not unaccustomed to vigorous and even violent criticism of my works and views. The fact is that my comments and interpretations have always been so independent that I have in my time been criticized by Chinese, Japanese, Germans, Russians, and Mongols, as well as by intemperate American writers. The criticisms run all the way from calling me an arch-imperialist to calling me a Red. But I assure you that none of this criticism has prevented me from writing the truth as I see it. And not even Senator McCarthy's criticism will prevent me from stating the facts and my views with all the honesty and vigor of which I am capable. I feel that this is peculiarly my obligation at this time, and the obligation of every other student and specialist who has the nation's interest at heart.

Having at last hacked my way through the jungle of McCarthy's charges, allegations, and threats, I wanted now to analyze the meaning of these vicious charges. In the foreground there are the unscrupulous ambitions of a shady politician willing to machine-gun his way to the front pages of the newspapers, reckless of any damage to the reputations of innocent persons, combined with the savage determination of fanatics and paid lobbyists working in the interests of a discredited, corrupt, and tottering foreign government. In the background, a sense of uneasiness and fear is spreading among the American people; a feeling that Asia is unknown and mysterious, but that something must have gone terribly wrong there. Out of this fear springs a growing, hysterical willingness to try to get rid of fear by finding a scapegoat. So I went on:

No man can state with absolute assurance what the future holds with respect to China. Various alternatives are apparent: First, some people still think it is conceivable that the National-ist Government in Formosa may reconquer China from the Communists. Second, it is possible that a middle-of-the-road or democratic group in China not necessarily part of the Na-tionalist Government — those whom General Marshall rightly called "a splendid group of men" — can still maintain their strong position in the confidence of the Chinese people unless we drive them completely into the hands of the Communists. Third, it is possible that the Chinese Communists will establish a regime which is Communist but substantially independent of the Soviet Union — what people loosely call Titoism. Fourth, it is possible that the Chinese Communist Government will be drawn more and more completely into the orbit of the Soviet Union and will become a satellite state.

There is one thing, and perhaps only one thing, that is perfectly clear. That is, that the fourth possibility — namely, complete and absolute absorption in fact of China by the Soviet Union — would be an unrelieved catastrophe for the United States and for the Chinese people. That means that our national policy must be to do everything that we can to bring about one of the other possibilities that I have stated: namely, to assist the Nationalist Government to reconquer China; to preserve China's independence of the Soviet Union even at the distasteful price of accepting a government of independent Chinese Communists; or to encourage the survival of the strong but unorganized middle group in China — not necessarily connected with the Nationalist Government — which might still be able to limit the power of the Communists and keep China on a road at least parallel to democracy in its internal life and its relations with the outside world.

Now, gentlemen, as I have said, I know of nothing that would be more helpful to our nation and our government than full and free debate on this most difficult and vitally important problem. I would myself exclude the first alternative altogether. It is my view that the Nationalist Government in Formosa cannot hope to recapture China, and that the large commitment of United States resources in the Formosa adventure would not merely be wasteful, but would be of positive assistance to the Soviet Union because it would make it possible and perhaps inevitable for the Chinese Communists to invite increased participation of the Soviet Union in the conflict.

Let me illustrate this. As the air assaults increase, with United States planes launched by the Nationalist forces from

Formosa upon the mainland of China, there is danger — if it is not already a fact — that the Chinese Communist Government with the backing of many of the Chinese people, will invite the Soviet Union to establish air bases and to engage actively in the air war. I personally believe that if the Soviet Union establishes air bases in China they will not be dismantled when the Nationalist forces are defeated. To me this is an appalling prospect. To me, this would make it probable if not certain that the die is cast — that the Chinese Government and the Chinese people will be subordinated to the Soviet Union for a long time to come.

Accordingly, it is my view that the major American effort must be in one of the other two directions: namely, to encourage a nationalism, even if it is Communist nationalism, capable of standing up to the Soviet Union and maintaining independence in its dealings with us, or to encourage in every possible way the conditions that will make possible the survival of a so-called third force, a democratic group within China, that can change the character of the government. It seems to me that our long-term objective should clearly be the latter, to build up conditions that favor a democratic group, including such elements of the Kuomintang as may be available and suitable. But it may be that in the short run, while working at this long-term objective, our first objective will have to be to avoid closing the trap on the Chinese so that they feel they have no alternative but Russia — even if it means temporizing with Titoism.

Now, gentlemen, my analysis of this may be partly or wholly wrong. But if anybody says that it is disloyal or un-American, he is a fool or a knave. But it is exactly this analysis which, I am sure, has provoked the current attack in which I have been called these preposterous and villainous names that have been uttered by Senator McCarthy.

Senator McCarthy, without, I am sure, knowing what he is about, has been and is the instrument or the dupe of a bitter and implacable and fanatical group of people who will not tolerate any discussion of China which is not based upon absolute, total and complete support of the Nationalist Government in Formosa. They do not hesitate at — they even insist on — policies that potential allies of ours in India, Indonesia, Pakistan, and other countries will call ruthless imperialism. Their conclusion — that is, that the United States should put all of its eggs in the Nationalist Government's basket — may be right or wrong. I think it's wrong.

But I am *sure* that the methods of that faction of these people who are McCarthy's Edgar Bergen, are wrong — as wrong as wrong can be. Their methods are to intimidate persons like me and even officials of the United States Government from expressing views that are contrary to their own. Their weapon of intimidation is McCarthy's machine gun: namely, accusation of disloyalty and traitorous conduct. I get a certain amount of wry amusement out of the fact that some of these people are acknowledged ex-Communists. Perhaps that status gives them a special right to criticize those of us who do not happen to be Communists, ex or otherwise. Certainly, it provides them with ideal training and unique skill for the kind of campaign of vilification and distortion that the so-called China Lobby is conducting through the instrumentality of the Senator from Wisconsin.

I do not, by what I have said, want to indicate a feeling of despair about the possibility of democratic success in China. I think I know the Chinese people reasonably well. I have not only great affection, but great admiration for them. Despite the relatively backward state of their country, the Chinese people have a strong and rugged sense of individualism and democracy. If they accept the restraints and repressions of

Communism, it will be because they feel that they have no alternative for national and individual survival. If they accept the iron dominion of world-wide Communism, it will be because we, the democratic nations and peoples of the world, have failed. It will be because we, by reason of ignorance or incompetence, have not presented them with an effective choice.

To date, that is exactly what has happened. We have failed in China. Senator McCarthy does me the honor of saying that I am the architect of this policy which has failed. Let me point out that even if this were so it would not be disloyalty. It would mean that I am a poor architect. The fact of the matter, however, is quite the contrary.

The fact is that I have never held a position in the United States Government in which I could make policy. The fact is that I have been very little consulted by those who do make policy — before Pearl Harbor, during the war, or since the war. I think I can fairly claim — with great regret — that I am the least consulted man of all those who have a public reputation in this country as specialists on the Far East.

Senator McCarthy has stated that United States Far Eastern policy, and especially China policy, has followed my recommendations "step for step." The record shows the exact opposite to be true. Before the war, I was in favor of a much tougher policy toward Japan than the State Department was willing to follow. During the war, I warned that we must be prepared for a period of very rapid change throughout Asia. No attention was paid to this warning. The last chapters of my book, *Solution in Asia*, published in 1945, a few months before the end of the war, are a crowded catalogue of unaccepted recommendations.

Since the war, my recommendations have had equally little influence on the State Department. The most recent example of this is my memorandum of last August to the State Department committee headed by Ambassador Jessup, whom Senator McCarthy has called "a Lattimore front." In this I warned that we cannot expect to succeed with little Chiang Kai-sheks where we failed with the big Chiang Kai-shek. But we are still supporting a little Chiang Kai-shek in South Korea and we have since taken on another one in Indo-China. I warned that we cannot coerce China by cutting off trade; but by our feeble attitude toward the blockade of Shanghai, we have allowed trade to be virtually cut off. I warned that by indecision in recognizing the facts of life in China we were heading for another setback in Asia without even the compensating advantage of hampering Russia's ability to maneuver in Europe; that is exactly what has happened. I warned that reliance on Japan as an instrument of American policy is a bad bet; but Japan is still our most risky bet in Asia. I warned that countries in the Far East must not be made to suspect that the real aim of the United States is to use them against Russia; but all of them are now convinced that this is just what our real aim is.

My recommendations may be right or wrong. I may be accused of having given bad advice by anyone who disagrees with my opinions. What I cannot be accused of is advice that has influenced the policy of the United States in the Far East. I wish that I had in fact had more influence. If I had, I think that the Communists would not now control China.

The very foundation of my views towards China is a firm belief that the United States and the democratic nations of the world — if they are willing to abandon the mistaken policies of the past and face the problems of China and the Far East realistically — can help to bring about the establishment of strong democratic governments in the Far East that will work harmoniously with the western powers. Despite Senator Mc-

Carthy, my books and articles witness that my basic beliefs are the absolute antithesis of the Marxist doctrine. The Communist line as applied to Asia may be easily summed up: The Communists say that Capitalism is in decay, and because it is in decay, the European empires are falling apart; capitalist nations in Europe and America are incapable of any nonimperialist relation with these former colonies which can, therefore, look for hope only to the Soviet Union.

In my view, this is nonsense. I believe that both capitalism and political democracy have immense vitality and adaptability. If they fail to survive, I believe it will be because of dogmatic or uninformed men who insist on policies of coercion, repression and inequality — not because of inherent defects in capitalism and democracy.

But I want to emphasize with all my heart, that we ourselves, if we are so foolish as to destroy our own democracy, can make the Marxist dream come true. We ourselves can cause the decay of capitalism and democracy. The sure way to do this is to permit the destruction of the basic wellspring from which capitalism and democracy derive their vitality: namely, freedom of research, freedom of speech, and freedom for men stoutly to maintain their diverse opinions.

I say to you, gentlemen, that the sure way to destroy freedom of speech and the free expression of ideas and views is to attach to that freedom the penalty of abuse and vilification. If the people of this country can differ with the so-called China Lobby or with Senator McCarthy only at the risk of the abuse to which I have been subjected, freedom will not long survive. If officials of our government cannot consult people of diverse views without exposing themselves to the kind of attack that Senator McCarthy has visited upon officers of the State Department, our governmental policy will necessarily be sterile. It is only from a diversity of views freely expressed and strongly advocated that sound policy is distilled. He who contributes to the destruction of this process is either a fool or an enemy of his country. Let Senator McCarthy take note of this.

Now, gentlemen, I shall be glad to answer any questions that you may care to ask.

While I had been reading, there was no scuffling or whispering in the crowded room. The only interruption had been the flaring up of the newsreel lights, which had been turned off only for very brief intervals, and the occasional disconcerting flash of press cameras, which always seemed to go off right in my left eye. I knew this statement so well that I could take my eyes off the page whenever I came to a sentence or two that I could repeat by heart. Whenever one of these opportunities came, I looked full at McCarthy. I was not surprised that he was not there in the afternoon.

When I had finished reading my statement, I was tired and sat back in my chair, but the suddenness and fervor of the applause startled me and made me sit up again. Senator Tydings smiled broadly as he rapped his gavel to restore order. He declared a brief recess, and I went out to the hall, where the air was less stuffy. One of the uniformed guards took me by the elbow and steered me out of the crowd. "Keep after him, boy," he said in a hoarse whisper in my ear; "you're doing fine!"

CHAPTER IV

THEN the hearing resumed, and the questioning began — and the politics. It was evident that the Democratic members hoped, at this moment, to get a quick and complete vindication and to wind up the "Lattimore case." It soon became equally plain, however, that Senator Hickenlooper feared that collapse of the charges against me would mean collapse of the whole "loyalty" campaign against the Department of State. The questions addressed to me by Senator McMahon and Senator Green were perfunctory. Senator Lodge was not there during the afternoon hearing. But Senator Hickenlooper set to work patiently on a long, slowly developed line of questioning which soon showed that he was determined to drag out the hearing, in the hope that a new line of attack might be developed.

His first questions were an attempt to treat all problems in China, and all my ideas about them, as if Communism were the only issue. What had been my "contact with Communist activities" during my "lifelong associations in the Orient and other places in the world?" He suggested that I had "become familiar with the methods" of Communists. What was my opinion of the methods of "Communism, as controlled from Moscow?" "Has it," he asked, "come to your knowledge or your belief in China that Russia has been attempting for a number of years to extend Communist influence?" Was it my opinion that the Chinese Communist leaders were "Moscow inspired or Moscow trained?"

Questions like these are more difficult for an expert to answer than for an ordinary newspaper reader. The longer a man has lived and studied in a country like China the more he is likely to realize that Communism is only one factor — though a potent and yeasty factor — in a vast confusion and interaction of other factors. To analyze and understand the problems of China it is as important to understand what Communism works on as it is to study how Communism works; just as anyone who wants to become an expert on baking bread should study the characteristics of different kinds of flour as well as the properties of yeast. All of my answers, therefore, were patiently directed toward establishing the fact that China is a country of many problems, not just one problem, and that "the main factor in the triumph of Communism in China was not the skill or willingness of the Chinese Communists, but rather the almost unbelievably gross mistakes of those who previously held power in China."

Hickenlooper then moved on to a favorite question of the China Lobby. Had I, from 1945 to 1947, supported "the theory that a coalition government should be formed in China, and that Communist representatives should be taken into the government?" I replied that I had. "In that respect I very closely followed and agreed with the opinions formed by General Marshall, summarized in his report to the President of January, 1947. If I may summarize, it appears to me that General Marshall went out to China and, with the quick eye of the magnificent strategic analyst that he is, he understood that he was in a situation in which salvation was impossible and salvage was all that could be hoped for. He therefore endeavored to salvage as much of the situation as he thought was possible with the resources of the National Government and the support of the United States Government. I do not think any man could have done an abler job. I am very sorry that he failed. Incidentally, I supported him whole-heartedly in his policy at that time when the Communists were vilifying him as a crook and double-dealer."

Hickenlooper tried to turn this aside by suggesting that General Marshall had made "the same recommendation" that Vice-President Wallace had made when he came back from China in 1944. I pointed out that I had not known what recommendations Mr. Wallace had brought back, but in the period when he was in Chungking "many Americans in our diplomatic and military services were becoming alarmed about the situation in the National Government of China. They were already afraid that the rot had gone so far that that government would not be able to capture the imagination of the people at the end of the war." Some of the warnings they were sending to Washington were later published in the famous White Paper on China. The men who wrote these warnings, I pointed out, "were intelligence officers doing exactly what the military and diplomatic services required of them, namely, finding out what the score was, instead of indulging in wishful thinking, and some of them I regret to say have been politically crucified for doing an honest job of work."

Senator Green tried vainly to make the point that this was supposed to be an investigation of disloyalty in the

State Department. Senator Tydings acknowledged this point, and acknowledged that I had had only "an auxiliary connection" with the State Department, but said that he would "lean over backwards lest we be charged, as we have been, with not wanting to bring in everything that is pertinent." And Hickenlooper then revealed his intention of plodding ahead with his gumshoe-and-magnifying-glass inquiry into my "views and opinions and the whole background." He also revealed the frame of mind of sullen suspicion in which he would conduct his inquiry. "The allegation is made," he said, "that he is an insidious fellow," and he therefore claimed the right to pursue his inquiry concerning me as far as he liked — which took him a long way from the Committee's mandate to examine the loyalty of people in the State Department.

When the questioning broke off for the noon recess, friends and strangers came crowding up. Senator Tom Connally, who had sat all through the morning, came over to shake hands and to say a word or two about the scandalously reckless nature of the McCarthy charges. As the crowd thinned, I had a chance to greet my mother and father. Eleanor, Paul Porter, Abe Fortas and I lunched at the Carlton, feeling gay and confident that the worst of the strain was over. When we went back to the Caucus Room at the Senate Office Building, Senator Tydings and the Dilowa Hutukhtu amicably posed for the photographers together.

Then Hickenlooper began his questioning again. One of the most important points that he tried to make that afternoon was an obvious booby trap: the Chinese Communists, as he presented the problem, want us to get out of

Formosa. Lattimore is warning us to get out of Formosa. Therefore Lattimore is following the Communist line. Owing to the fact that so few people know the details of the pattern of politics in Asia, this kind of apparently logical but really deceptive grouping of facts can be made to sound very ominous, but the truth is very different. The basic fact about Formosa is that the remnants of Chiang Kai-shek's government and army will not be able to hold it for very long, while we, if we were to allow ourselves to be "sucked in" to try to hold it as an American advance base would soon find it a source of more weakness than strength. We would not, in the twentieth century, be able to control China from Formosa as the British, under the very different conditions of the nineteenth century, once controlled a large part of China from Hong Kong. Continued American support of the rump government on Formosa, rejected by its own people, would be a rejection of the basic principle of government by the consent of the governed, and would be a deadly blow to our prestige in countries like India, Pakistan, Indonesia, and Afghanistan. People in those countries would be convinced that we had turned imperialistic, and instead of being friendly toward us they would become afraid of us.

In this situation, the Russians and the Chinese Communists keep up a loud propaganda demanding that we "get out of Formosa." It may very well be, however, that they hope we will try not to abandon Chiang Kai-shek and Formosa, because the longer we hang on the greater and more damaging will be our "loss of face" when we finally do have to let go. People like myself — and there are quite a few of us — believe, for the reasons I have just given, that there is a danger that we may damage our position in the much more important countries of Asia by trying to support Chiang Kai-shek and to hold on to Formosa. If we are right in this opinion, then we are also right in advising that we abandon Chiang Kai-shek and Formosa sooner rather than later. If it is advisable to leave a place, then it is advisable to do so early enough so that it is quite plain that you are leaving with dignity and by a decision of your own.

The argument that in abandoning Chiang we would be abandoning "our wartime ally" — a favorite phrase of the China Lobby — is nonsense. Our wartime ally was the Chinese nation. At the end of the war Chiang, in spite of sound advice from General Marshall and other Americans, forfeited the confidence of that nation, and the last thing we could hope to do would be to win back the confidence of the nation by foisting on them the man they have rejected.

Hickenlooper's big bombshell of the afternoon — or intended bombshell — was a letter, which he produced from among his papers, which he said was supposed to have been written by me in June 1943, as director of Pacific Operations of the Office of War Information in San Francisco, to Joseph Barnes who was then Director of Atlantic Operations of the Office of War Information in New York. It was an unsigned file copy, marked "secret," and he dramatically handed it to me to identify. This was obviously the letter McCarthy had referred to in his Senate speech in which he claimed that I had "ordered" Barnes to "fire from the O.W.I. any man who is loyal to Chiang, and hire individuals who are loyal to the Communist government." I had replied in my statement that morning that if there were such a letter Senator McCarthy had certainly completely distorted its meaning. So I was very curious to see the letter.

As soon as I had the letter in my hands, and had read enough of it to identify it, I demanded that the whole text be put into the record. Hickenlooper had handed it to me only to make me acknowledge that it was genuine, but had thought that he could withhold it from the public record on security grounds, because it was a classified document, so that the public would still know nothing about it except from McCarthy's maliciously distorted quotations. Hickenlooper now tried to double-talk himself out of revealing the text but he had lost control of the situation. On the one hand he said, "I personally feel that inasmuch as the letter was referred to the entire letter should, if properly eligible to be made public, be put in the record"; on the other hand he said that "I do not want to violate an existing secret classification." Later, when he saw that he was losing ground and that the text of the letter was likely to be revealed, he appealed to the timidity about classified documents that frequently keeps Administration supporters on the defensive. "I would suggest," he said, "before the Chairman undertakes the responsibility of declassifying a matter that is legally classified that he ought to think it over a bit."

As a matter of fact, Senator Tydings need not have worried about the problem of declassification. I found out later that the letter had been used as long ago as 1948 by Kohlberg, in a magazine article in *China Monthly* — and used with exactly the same distortion that McCarthy later used, creating a strong presumption that the letter came into McCarthy's hands from Kohlberg. How did this fanatical member of the China Lobby come to have access to, or to have in his possession, a classified document of the American Government? It seems to me extraordinary that this question has never been followed up or investigated.

In any case, after some amusing byplay Senator Tydings did take the responsibility of declassifying the letter and asking Mr. Fortas to read it aloud. He read as follows:

In your capacity as a member of our Personnel Security Committee there are certain things which you ought to know about Chinese personnel. It is a delicate matter for me to tell you about these things because of my recent official connection with Generalissimo Chiang Kai-shek. For that reason I am marking this communication secret.

When we recently reduced the number of our Chinese staff in New York it was quite obvious that there was going to be trouble and that this trouble would take the form of accusations against the remaining personnel. The fact is that certain of the personnel with whose services we dispensed had connections outside the office. This leads directly into the main question. It is extremely important from the point of view of security that intelligence information should not leak out of our office through our Chinese personnel. It is an open secret in Washington that the security of various Chinese agencies there is deplorable. Any pipeline from our office to any of those agencies is not a pipeline but practically an open conduit.

However, it is not only a question of Chinese government agencies. There is also a well organized and well financed organization among the Chinese in this country connected with Wang Ching-wei, the Japanese puppet. This can be traced back to the history of the Chinese

Revolution as a whole. To present it in the fewest possible words: Sun Yat-sen was largely financed for many years by Chinese living abroad. Not only Sun Yat-sen but Wang Ching-wei had close connections among the overseas Chinese. However much he is a traitor now the fact must be recognized that Wang Ching-wei is a veteran of Chinese politics with connections which he has nourished for many years among Chinese communities abroad, including those in the United States.

Chinese in the United States come almost exclusively from a few localities on the coast of China, practically every one of which is now occupied by the Japanese. Thus these Chinese in America have both family connections and financial investments which are under the control of the Japanese, and because of his years of political organizing work Wang Ching-wei knows all of these connections and can apply pressure through them.

On the other side there is a special organization within the Kuomintang or Chinese Nationalist Party at Chungking which is charged with maintaining political and financial connections with Chinese overseas. This Overseas Bureau also has a detailed knowledge of the Chinese communities in America and is able to apply pressure. Thus there is a very intense conflict going on every day in every Chinatown in America between the Wang Ching-wei agents and those of the Kuomintang. It must be remembered that while the Kuomintang is able to operate in a private way as a political party among Chinese residents in America, it is also the party which "owns" the Chinese Government and is thus able to make use of Chinese Government agencies.

Thirdly, there are numerous Chinese in America who are politically unaffiliated. There are, of course, Communists but they have neither the money nor the organization of the Wang Ching-wei and Kuomintang groups. The genuinely unaffiliated Chinese are a curious compound product of Chinese politics and American environment. They tend to be intensely loyal to China as a country, without conceiving that the Kuomintang or any other political organization has a monopoly right to control of their thoughts and actions. They are like Americans; they like to give their political allegiance, not to have it demanded of them. They are reluctant to support a regimented series of causes laid down for them under orders; like Americans, they often give moral and financial support to a scattered number of causes, some of which may even conflict with each other to a certain extent.

The conflict between the Wang Ching-wei organizing group and the Kuomintang organizing group in America cannot be fought out in the open. Both sides have very good reasons for not courting publicity. Each is anxious to bring into its fold as many of the unaffiliated Chinese as possible. Each is also anxious not to be exposed as an "un-American" organization or a foreign political group working on American soil. Both of them accordingly find it very good tactics, not only to cover up themselves but to put pressure on those whom they are trying to bring under their control, to accuse unaffiliated Chinese of being Communists. This is an accusation which covers up the accuser at the same time that it puts pressure on the accused.

One of the outstanding rallying points of the unaffiliated Chinese in America is the *New China Daily News* in New York. This is controlled by an organization of laundrymen. I understand that the shareholders number two or three thousand and that they take an active interest in the newspaper. The essential thing about these laundrymen is that in the nature of their business they are independent small businessmen. This means that they are on the one hand fairly well insured against Communist ideology, since the small businessman of whatever nationality is likely to be a man who had made his way by his own initiative and enterprise and is therefore extremely suspicious of collectivist economic theories. On the other hand these Chinese small business proprietors are reluctant to submit themselves unquestioningly to the control of the vested interests which have grown up in China in association with the dominant Kuomintang. The *New China Daily News* would probably not come under much pressure if it were not for the fact that it is one of the best edited Chinese papers in America with a growing circulation. It does not need to be subsidized or supported by a patron, like many, perhaps the majority, of Chinese papers. It pays dividends on its own merits. A number of Chinese-language papers in America receive subsidies from the Kuomintang. At least two, and perhaps three, receive subsidies from the Wang Ching-wei group. One or two others trace back to the group within the Kuomintang which was at one time headed by the late Hu Han-min, a leader of the right-wing faction within the Kuomintang. The Hu Han-min group, though once regarded as right-wing conservatives, are now regarded in China as "old-fashioned liberals" — liberal, so to speak, short of the New Deal. They are less bitterly involved in Chinatown politics than the Wang Ching-wei and Kuomintang groups. The two latter, which are engaged in handing out carefully colored news and doctored editorial policies, are intensely jealous of and hostile to an unaffiliated paper like the *New China Daily News*, which, so to speak, flaunts its sins by being so readable that the Chinese public in America buys it for its own sake.

It would be rash to say that there are no Communists connected with the *New China Daily News*. Here it is necessary to consider another peculiarity of the politics of Chinese living out of China. These Chinese are far from being tied to the chariot wheels of Moscow; but when it comes to resisting the trend toward totalitarian regimentation within China they are often willing to support parts of the program advocated by the Chinese Communists within China. This is so much a part of the pattern of politics of Chinese living out of China that it is not uncommon to find wealthy men, even millionaires, supporting the program of the Chinese Communists in whole or in part. This was, for instance, conspicuous in Malaya before the fall of Singapore. For such prosperous and independent Chinese it was a question either of backing their independent judgment of the steps that needed to be taken toward creating a working democracy within China, or of paying financial tribute to the Kuomintang, which sometimes tends to be autocratic, and not infrequently spurns advice from Chinese abroad at the same time that it demands their financial contributions.

In the specific setting of America, it is the independent small businessman — like the laundryman — rather than the very few wealthy merchants who most conspicuously maintain this tradition of political independence. In America, some of the most wealthy individuals are either committed to Wang Ching-wei and his puppet Japanese party or at least are hedging until they have a better idea of how the war is finally going to turn out.

In the circumstances we have to be extremely careful about our Chinese personnel. While we need to avoid recruiting any Chinese Communists we must be careful not to be frightened out of hiring people who have loosely been accused of being Communists. We have to be at least equally careful of not hiring people who are pipelines to the Wang Ching-wei or to one or other of the main factions within the Kuomintang. After all, as an American Government agency we should deal with the Chinese Government or regular agencies of the Chinese Government, but should not get in the position of committing ourselves to the Kuomintang, the political party which controls the Chinese Government, as if it were itself the Chinese Government. You will recognize the importance of this proposition and the delicacy which it requires on the operation level.

For our purposes, it is wise to recruit as many unaffiliated Chinese as we can, to pick people whose loyalty will be reasonably assured on the one hand by the salaries which we pay them and on the other hand by the fact that they do not receive salaries or subsidies from somewhere else.

Dr. Chi and Mr. Chew Hong, both of our New York office, conform excellently to these requirements. Dr. Chi I have known for many years. Until his family estates were occupied by the Japanese, he was a wealthy landlord. He was brought up in the older scholastic tradition in China, before the spread of modern Western education, but at the same time he is keenly interested in the national unification of China and the orderly development of a stable political organization there. I know by long experience that he is anything but a Communist; I also know that because of his seniority, his background of independent wealth, and his superior mentality he is not a man to be pushed around by party bureaucrats. Chew Hong is a much younger man, but one whom Dr. Chi trusts and of whose integrity he is convinced. There is something in their relationship of the old Chinese standards of disciple and master. As long as Dr. Chi stands in the relationship of loyal friendship to me and the loyalty of an honest employee of an American government agency, there will be no difficulty with either man, no irresponsible playing with Chinese politics, and no leakage to any Chinese faction.

The retention of both men is therefore a guarantee to the secrecy and security of the work of the O.W.I. as well as a guarantee of the confident fulfillment of directives. I urge you not to be high-pressured into getting rid of either man. I know that both men may be subjected to attacks. Given time to work on it, I could undoubtedly trace such attacks to their origin and give you the full details. I doubt whether the Personnel Security Committee of O.W.I. would be able to trace such attacks, rooted in the intricacies of Chinese factional politics, to their source; but I should not like to see us placed in a position where, after getting rid of people now attacked, we would be forced to hire people who would actually be the nominee of factions not under our control.

It is for this reason that I have written this long letter to urge you to report to our Personnel Security Committee the necessity for exercising pronounced agnosticism when any of our Chinese personnel are attacked.

In the meantime I am doing my best to check over our Chinese personnel in San Francisco.

Once more I urge you to observe the strictest confidence in acting on this letter, because in certain quarters it might be considered that I am under a moral obligation to see that O.W.I. is staffed with Chinese who take their orders from some source other than the American Government.

Yours,
OWEN LATTIMORE
Director of Pacific Operations

The reading of the full text of the letter put me in the clear. It was also dramatic proof of the conscienceless extremes to which McCarthy would go in twisting a quotation into a lying accusation. Instead of "ordering" Joe to hire individuals loyal to the Communist government, I had specifically written a routine and matter-of-course warning that "we need to avoid recruiting any Chinese Communists."

Actually the letter was a guide, valuable to our security personnel at the time, on the intricate politics of Chinese factions in America. The background which had produced the letter was a routine problem of the war years. We had to maintain a strict watch to see that our foreign-born personnel, who spoke the languages of the countries to which we were broadcasting, were controlled only by the American Government and not by political groups in their home countries. In the case of Chinese personnel, this raised personal problems for me, because of course all Chinese were aware of my recent connection with Chiang Kai-shek. I therefore wanted to make sure that our personnel, while loyal to Chiang, were not controlled by the Kuomintang.

In this, I was following the standard government policy. We had to support our allies, but to avoid getting mixed

up in their domestic politics. On our broadcasts we praised
Churchill, for example, as the wartime leader of Britain, but
never spoke of him as the leader of the Conservative Party.
We supported Stalin, as the wartime leader of Russia, but
did not advertise Communism by referring to him as the
leader of the Russian Communists. I had written my colleague in New York that I relied on the loyalty of old
Dr. Chi, whom I knew to be thoroughly free of Marxism
and Communism. I had also known his son, during the
early 1930's in New York and in 1941 and 1942 in Chungking where he held a high position in the Bank of China
and was very much in the confidence of Dr. H. H. Kung,
then Chinese Minister of Finance.

After the war Dr. Chi had gone back to China as a
professor in a Kuomintang-controlled university in Peking.
When the Communists took over Peking, he stayed on
— as did most of the university professors. Later it was
reported that his son had entered the service of the new
Communist-controlled government — but so did many other
high officials formerly in the Kuomintang government.
McCarthy had made a great hullabaloo, as if these changes
in the lives of Chinese far away in China, years later, proved
me to have Communist connections; but such things happen
to people living in countries going through revolutions,
and in any case could not be either prevented or promoted
by an American professor living in Baltimore.

Hickenlooper's attempted maneuver had been so outrageous, and it was so clear that McCarthy had already
violated security in quoting from the letter, and that Hickenlooper had no business having the document in his possession that Senators Tydings and Green began to needle him

on the obvious fact that either he had got the letter from McCarthy or he and McCarthy had got it from the same unauthorized source. Hickenlooper, trying to talk his way out, lost his temper.

After the failure of his attempted bombshell, the rest of Senator Hickenlooper's questions were rather inconsequential. The steam had gone out of him, and he seemed only to be going through motions in order to keep the hearing going until five o'clock.

Finally, Senator Tydings stood up, and smiling like a man who is about to produce a Christmas present said:

"Dr. Lattimore, your case has been designated as the No. 1 case, finally, in the charges made by Senator McCarthy. You have been called, substantially, I think, if not accurately quoting, the top Red spy agent in America. We have been told that if we had access to certain files that this would be shown.

"I think as chairman of this committee that I owe it to you and to the country to tell you that four of the five members of this committee, in the presence of Mr. J. Edgar Hoover, the head of the F.B.I., had a complete summary of your file made available to them. Mr. Hoover himself prepared those data. It was quite lengthy. And at the conclusion of the reading of that summary in great detail, it was the universal opinion of all of the members of the committee present, and all others in the room, of which there were two more, that there was nothing in that file to show that you were a Communist or had ever been a Communist, or that you were in any way connected with any espionage information or charges, so that the F.B.I. file puts you completely, up to this moment, at least, in the clear."

I couldn't see Eleanor, who was sitting right behind me, but Abe, sitting beside me, dropped his hand on my arm. It was a moment of exhilaration so great that for a moment I forgot that it was not vindication — that in a democracy a man's standing as a citizen should not depend on his secret police file. McCarthyism tends to create such a false standard, but accepting it means the end of our democracy.

It was clear, nevertheless, that Senator Tydings was doing his best within the limits of the situation created by McCarthy to announce the fact that he was convinced that McCarthy's charges against me had been unfounded. His smile got wider and wider until, as we used to say when we were children, it went right round his head and tied in a bowknot behind.

The klieg lights went off, and I realized they had been on so long that my face felt sunburned. At last I could stand up, turn around, and see Eleanor. The cameramen wanted us to fall into each other's arms, but we just held hands. David came up and stood by us, possessively. My mother and father were not there. They had gone home at noon, tired out.

To celebrate, we went to Abe's to listen to the radio commentators and watch the television newsreel, and then out to a wonderful dinner at La Salle du Bois. Everything looked and felt like a smashing victory.

CHAPTER V

THE EXHILARATION lasted for two days. The accounts of
the hearing had gone out all over the country, not only
to the press and radio, but by television and newsreels.
There was no doubt whatever that the national response
had been favorable. An early indication came when, as I
finished reading my statement at my hearing, a man at the
press table, representing a paper whose editors could be
counted on to back McCarthy, no matter how wild his
antics, turned around to Abe Fortas and said "How in the
hell am I to handle this one?" Again, when I bought a
ticket to go up to Philadelphia, the ticket seller recognized
me and said "I saw you in the newsreel. Nice job." When
I went into a post office to buy stamps, I got almost the
same greeting. And on trains, complete strangers would
stop me and shake hands.

My father, who has always been devoted to the classics,
paid me his most courtly compliment, comparing my statement to Cicero's oration against Catiline. But what Eleanor
and I liked most was David's support. A nineteen-year-old
son is at the age when none of his parents' defects are
hidden from him. David didn't ask for any exciting or spec-
tacular jobs. He stood by and was willing to do whatever
was wanted, whenever it was wanted. And I had the finest

and proudest feeling a father can have — the complete approval and support of my son.

Tired, but feeling we had won the battle, we packed up an enormous load of books and files in the back of our Plymouth Suburban, and drove home to Ruxton to rest. But though we had won a battle, there was still a campaign to fight.

McCarthy's gamble, against me as against Ambassador Jessup and others, had been to make accusations first and hope the proof would turn up later. Having lost the gamble, he now doubled the stakes. In one of his statements from the Senate floor, before I returned from Afghanistan, he had said that he would produce a witness who would testify that I was or had been a "Communist, under Communist discipline." The press speculated that he must mean Louis F. Budenz, the sensational ex-Communist author and lecturer. Subsequently, however, nothing happened, and we had begun to think that either McCarthy for some reason was afraid to produce Budenz, or Budenz for some reason was unwilling to appear. Budenz said in a press interview in the Middle West that he had never met McCarthy. In a few days, however, it looked as if in one way or another the heat had been turned on. It was announced that Budenz had been subpoenaed, and would appear.

I had known practically nothing about Budenz except that I had heard of him as a man who had turned a sordid past into a lucrative present of writing and lecturing. I soon learned that he was also a man who had built up a morbid and almost hypnotic reputation as a kind of "finger of doom." It seems that in the early period after he got out of the Communist Party, Budenz had helped the authorities to uncover a couple of sensational Communist figures — Gerhardt Eisler, and Sam Carr, who was involved in the Canadian spy ring. That, however, apparently exhausted his "hot" inside information. Since then he had been demoted to a secondary or "me too" informer. He was considered a great authority on the "apparatus" of Communist organization, and in later trials and Congressional hearings he had been thrown in as a makeweight; that is, in the case of a man already identified by somebody else as a Communist, or in the case of people already publicly known to be Communists, he had been brought in as a supplementary witness to testify that he also knew them or knew of them as Communists. This shift from informer first-grade to informer second-grade had, however, escaped public notice. As far as the general public was concerned, he had a reputation as an infallible authority on everything Communist. So now when it was announced that he would testify, with the expectation that he would in some way implicate me as a Communist, the front pages of the newspapers were smothered with huge banner headlines.

We packed up and moved back to Washington. When we got to the office I saw immediately that Abe was worried. He shut his door behind us, looked at me squarely, and said nothing for what seemed like a long, long time. Then he said, "McCarthy is a long way out on a limb. The political pressures that are building up are terrific. The report that Budenz will testify against you has shaken everyone in Washington. It is my duty as your lawyer to warn you that the danger you face cannot possibly be exaggerated. It does not exclude the possibility of a straight frame-up, with perjured witnesses and perhaps even forged documents. You have a choice of two ways of facing this danger. You can either take it head on, and expose yourself to this danger; or you can make a qualified and carefully guarded statement which will reduce the chance of entrapment by fake evidence. As your lawyer I cannot make that choice for you. You have to make it yourself."

"Abe," I said, "I don't see how we can do any pussyfooting on this. I want to meet this thing head on and slug it out. I owe it to myself and the issues that are at stake." Then I turned to Eleanor. I said, "Do you agree?" And she said, "Of course." Abe said nothing, but I could see from his face that I now had more than a lawyer. I had a friend, and we believed in each other.

Since Budenz was on a lecture tour and sent word that he could not appear until the following week, we had another day or two at home. I was also able to go up to Philadelphia for a day to give the closing address at the annual meeting of the American Academy of Political and Social Science, on problems of our foreign policy connected with President Truman's Point Four Program. The invitation to give this address had come after McCarthy's attack, and it was a mark of confidence that I deeply appreciated. I have never spoken to a more deeply attentive audience, and the prolonged applause both before I spoke and after I had finished was unmistakably intended to encourage me.

Returning to Washington, it was difficult to prepare for the Budenz hearing because there was no way of knowing what this man of sinister melodrama was going to say. There was a widespread report that he would claim that Frederick V. Field had told him either that I was a Communist Party member or that I had been useful to the Party. Abe therefore telephoned to Field, whom he traced to Nevada, and Field immediately responded with letters in which he said flatly that any statement that he had told Budenz anything at all about me would be a lie. Abe also followed up other leads which came to him during the week, including one which resulted in our getting an affidavit from an ex-Communist who had been higher in party circles than Budenz had been, a woman named Bella V. Dodd.

The story of how we got the affidavit shows how, in a battle like this, complete strangers sometimes come to your aid.

One night in New York Wellington Roe, an old-time labor organizer and writer for labor papers, went to the movies. There he saw a newsreel of my hearing in Washington. He told me afterwards that when he came out of the movie he said to himself "This guy is putting up a real fight. I've got to get in on it." I know very little about the labor movement — less, I am ready to admit, than a well-informed citizen ought to know. Up to this point I had never heard of Mr. Roe. But, as he explained to me when we met, in the turbulent history of the labor movement some people have moved to the left and others to the right — and some, of course, move back again. Thus a man who has been a long time in the movement, like Mr. Roe, is sure to have contacts with people of widely varying political views.

Among the people that Mr. Roe knew was Dr. Bella Dodd, who after many years of contact with labor unions had become a Communist and later was expelled from the

Communist Party. Mr. Roe remembered that she had once been a member of the top committee of the Communist Party and that for part of this time Budenz had been a member of the same committee. So he went to see her and was not surprised to find that in all her experience in the Communist Party she had never heard me mentioned — as a member, secret member, fellow traveler, sympathizer, or person whose writings were recommended to Party members. He then wrote this information to Senator Tydings and also to Abe Fortas.

When Abe got this letter, only a few days before Budenz was to testify, he quickly checked, through the Department of Labor and the Department of Justice, on both Mr. Roe and Dr. Dodd. He satisfied himself that Mr. Roe was a responsible person, and learned that Dr. Dodd really had been an important person in the Communist Party, and really had been expelled from it. He then telephoned Mr. Roe to see if he could persuade Dr. Dodd to come down for an interview. At first Mr. Roe thought he could arrange it, but then found that Dr. Dodd was quite unwilling to come. She had stood her ground on questions of principle in challenging the leadership of the Communist Party, and after being expelled had been subjected to personal attack by the Communists. Her law business had suffered, and though she bitterly resented the way in which the Communists had treated her, she dreaded the publicity that would be turned on her if she were to testify as an ex-Communist.

Finally, only the last afternoon before Budenz was to appear as a witness, Abe Fortas went up to New York to see her. The way he put the problem to her was that, as an ex-Communist who had been subjected to Communist attacks, she was in a unique position to understand my position as a man unjustly accused of Communism. She had stood up to the Communists on questions of principle. I was standing up to McCarthy on questions of principle. Abe told me that he said to her, "You are going to find it hard to live with yourself if Lattimore is successfully framed. You will never be able to forget that you might have helped by exposing the lies told against him. Or put it the other way round. If he wins out, you will always regret that you did not join in a good fight well fought." Abe told her frankly that while we would not ask to have her subpoenaed as a witness, there was a chance that the Committee itself might subpoena her. Knowing that there was this possibility, and knowing, as a lawyer, that if she appeared in public as an ex-Communist witness some of the cross-questioning would be brutally rough, she nevertheless had the courage to sign an affidavit in order to prevent injustice being done to a man who was a total stranger to her. Late at night Abe flew back from New York with the affidavit.

The best move we made that week, however, was to get in touch with Brigadier-General Elliott R. Thorpe, a retired Army officer whom I had known in Japan. Before I had got back from Afghanistan, he had written to Eleanor from Florida saying that he and his wife were about to drive to Minnesota to see a sister of his, but that he would be glad to do anything he could to help. He had been Chief of General MacArthur's Counter-Intelligence during the war in the Pacific, and before that had been in military intelligence work for many years in many parts of Asia.

After the occupation of Japan, and during the period I was there in the winter of 1945–46, he headed General MacArthur's Civil Intelligence. I had got to know him at that time. We had a good many differences of opinion — for instance, General Thorpe had a much higher opinion of the Dutch as colonial rulers than I did — but each of us was perfectly blunt about his own opinions, and each of us respected the other man's opinions and expert knowledge. Subsequently, General Thorpe had visited us in Ruxton. Later he had commanded an army school, then he had gone out as military attaché to our embassy in Thailand, and now he had retired from the army and was back in America for good. After writing to Eleanor, he had telegraphed to Senator Tydings as follows:

AS CHIEF OF ARMY COUNTER INTELLIGENCE OPERATIONS IN THE FAR EAST DURING AND AFTER THE WAR, I CAN STATE OWEN LATTIMORE GAVE VALUABLE ASSISTANCE OF A CONFIDENTIAL NATURE IN OUR OPERATIONS PROTECTING U.S. POLICIES FROM COMMUNIST DETECTION AND SABOTAGE. I PERSONALLY SUPERVISED CHECKING OF DOCTOR LATTIMORE'S OWN RELATIONSHIP AND OPINIONS RELATIVE TO THE U.S.S.R. HE WAS FOUND TO BE A LOYAL AMERICAN. AS THE RESULTS OF MY INVESTIGATIONS OF LATTIMORE, I ALSO FOUND HE HAD GAINED THE ANTIPATHY OF A LARGE NUMBER OF "OLD CHINA HANDS" BY HIS REALISTIC APPROACH TO THE ASIATIC PROBLEMS. IT IS MY BELIEF OWEN LATTIMORE IS A LOYAL CITIZEN.

We now remembered this telegram. With a highly publicized informer like Budenz on the stand, McCarthy would have everything going his way unless we could get in, on the same day, such an important witness as a high Army

Intelligence officer who had actually made an investigation of me.

To get away from our telephone, which we thought was probably tapped, I went over to a friend's house and called long distance to Minnesota. I found his sister, with whom he had been staying, but learned that he had gone to see another sister in Wisconsin. I traced him there and finally got him on the phone. I told him what was up. His voice over the phone sounded exactly like the kind of man he is. "Lattimore," he said, "I'm a soldier, even though I'm a retired soldier. This is a filthy dirty business, and for the good of the service, I don't want to get into it, one little bit. But if it's a question of truth and justice, I'll be down."

General Thorpe's standards are strict. When he got to Washington, he asked for a typewriter, shut himself in a room, and hammered out every word of his statement by himself. There was to be no question of consultation with either me or Abe Fortas. And he would not accept the hospitality of a hotel room or even a single meal. He stayed by himself until he appeared to give his testimony. He wanted it to be quite clear that there was no possibility of "undue influence."

I think people may be amused to know why it was that we thought our telephone was tapped. McCarthy, in one of his earlier excursions into the fantastic on the Senate floor, had attempted to prove that the Dilowa Hutukhtu, the distinguished Living Buddha from Outer Mongolia, who is working with me at the Johns Hopkins, is a fraud and an impostor and has never been in Outer Mongolia. In pursuit, presumably, of hot news about subversive collusion between me and my old Mongol friend — who incidentally was accused in a state trial in Outer Mongolia as a dangerous counterrevolutionary, and has spent a great many years of his life escaping from the Reds, first in one part of Asia and then in another — McCarthy got hold of a tape recording of a long conversation between me and the Dilowa Hutukhtu. This, apparently, he was peddling around Washington, hoping against hope to find someone who could translate it from Mongol into English. The news naturally got around to me, since inquiries about translation from Mongol into English are likely to get to me sooner or later, and I passed the word on to the Dilowa, who was delighted by the humor of the situation, and suggested that he ought to accept the translating job — for a suitable fee of course — but should then translate the recording from Mongol into Tibetan, since he doesn't speak English.

We were not thinking of jokes, however, when we went to the hearing room on April 20 to hear what Budenz had to say. Once more the room was so crowded that it seemed as if the walls would begin to bulge outward. Eleanor, Thurman Arnold, Abe Fortas, and I sat in chairs just back of where Budenz would sit. He came in late. He was a stocky man, partly nervous and partly self-assured. After he had taken the oath, he sat down with his back to me and I could not see his face any more. McCarthy was there again that morning, sitting back of the Committee table. Again he would not meet my eye. He looked tense and nervous, as if not sure that his witness would deliver the goods.

Budenz began his testimony. He was not reading from a

prepared statement, but seemed to have some notes and to be relying largely on memory and improvisation. As he rambled along, a nightmare seemed to be closing in on me. As in a nightmare, there were traces or echoes here and there of familiar things, which only made all the more strange and dreadful the other, unbelievable things that he was saying. Before long, the nightmare began to come into focus somewhat, and I recognized what it was that seemed familiar. Budenz, although he was supposed to be revealing new facts from his Communist past that he had hitherto kept hidden, was actually repeating old and long-disproved allegations that had been circulated for years by the China Lobby. It was not surprising that later, under questioning, he admitted not only his acquaintance with Alfred Kohlberg, but the fact that he had "lately" discussed me with Kohlberg. He also admitted that he had conferred in "the last couple of days" with ex-Congressman Charles J. Kersten, of Wisconsin, one of McCarthy's most active agents.

A great part of what Budenz had to say, however, consisted of long passages about the conspiratorial nature and organization of the Communist Party in America; its interpenetration and manipulation by agents sent from Russia; the way in which it was linked up with plots for sabotage and espionage.

These discursive reminiscences had nothing whatever to do with the proper functions of the subcommittee of the Senate Foreign Relations Committee, which had been set up for the specific purpose of inquiring into the loyalty records of specific individuals in the Department of State, accused by McCarthy. It had still less relevance to me personally, since I had never had any contact whatsoever with the murky world of Communist conspiracy. Yet as an emotional device for building up an atmosphere in a room, the recital was hypnotically effective.

The crowd at this hearing was very different from the one at my hearing two weeks before. On the day I made my statement, I had made no attempt to invite my friends, and only a sprinkling of people were there because they knew me or believed in me. The overwhelming majority were strangers. I had the feeling when I began of people who were listening with intense curiosity, but not with a partisan feeling in my favor. At the press tables, especially, the dead-pan expressions of the reporters were as good as a printed notification that they were not going to allow themselves to be swayed sentimentally in favor of a mere professor, with no political backing, pinned against a wall by a swashbuckling politician. Consequently, when I had set out my case and carried the attack to McCarthy himself, the effect was that of winning an argument and convincing strangers who had not come prepared to be convinced.

The mood of the crowd that had come to listen to Budenz was quite different. There was a strong representation of Catholic priests, whose black garb made them stand out conspicuously. It also happened that in the interval since my hearing a D.A.R. convention had assembled in Washington, with the result that in the crowd there was a high proportion of middle-aged and elderly women.

Budenz went on and on. His voice was that of a seasoned melodramatic performer, unctuous one moment and sinister the next. His plan of attack was simple. Early in his testimony he said that high Communists, whose names he gave as Earl Browder and Frederick V. Field, had said in his presence that I was under Communist discipline and that my assignment was to organize writers to put over stories to lull the American public into the belief that the Chinese Communists were not dangerous revolutionaries but just a bunch of well-meaning reformers. Then, to bolster this unlikely yarn, he deployed this attack into an enveloping movement.

First, he drew on his memories of his conspiratorial days to build up a frightening picture of a never-never land of Communist plotting and intrigue in which things are always the opposite of what they seem. Questioning exposed the fact that he had read only one of my books and that one hastily and recently. Shifting away from this weak point, he came up with a glib story of how, in the Communist world, a Communist agent may be shielded by special indulgences and dispensations permitting him to attack Communist ideas and the Party line. Thus, he warned, anything anti-Communist in either my writings or my actions ought to be taken as proof of my being in fact a Communist!

Second, he tried to dodge his inability to produce a supporting witness either among ex-Communists or people who are still Communists, by warning his hearers that Communists lie on principle. Anyone who came forward to contradict him would be a liar. Only the unsupported word of Louis F. Budenz could be taken as gospel.

Third, he stated flatly that the Communists bring libel actions in order to frighten people. Thus, if a man is called a Communist and does not defend himself, he is obviously a Communist. But if he brings a libel action, that also proves him to be a Communist.

Fourth, he thickened the atmosphere of underworld plots and menaces with a story of secret documents, circulated among high Communists, typed on onionskin paper. In such documents, he said, I was identified as L or XL. Don't count on any of these documents turning up, however. Budenz says they were so secret that immediately after being read they had to be torn up and flushed down the toilet.

This rigmarole of skulduggery, built up with repeated "I was there" allusions to his conspiratorial past, was extraordinarily effective as a psychological device for hypnotizing the attention of the people in the room.

Since Budenz was not reading a prepared statement, he was frequently interrupted by questions. After each of these questions, he would start off in a slightly new direction, and a great deal of the time he talked like a man reciting something he had learned by heart. I found the explanation of this when I got hold of a copy of his book, *This Is My Story*, the next day. This book was published five years ago, but evidently it still forms his stock in trade as a lecturer, because big chunks of it reappeared in his testimony. Sprinkled over the gravel of these stale recollections, like nuggets in a mine that has been "salted" in order to sell stock to suckers, were a few new allegations that he had never made before in his hundreds of hours of reporting to the F.B.I. or in his many appearances in a period of five years as a star witness in court cases and before Congressional committees.

His most circumstantial allegation was that he had heard

other Communists describe me as "organizing writers" to deceive the American public. When Senator Lodge asked him for "a specific instance when an order or an instruction" was given to me and carried out by me, he replied that "the order to represent the Chinese Communists as agrarian reformers was certainly carried out," but "specifically I do not know because I did not hear the detailed report on the matter." "Is that the most concrete and specific illustration there is?" Senator Lodge then asked. "That is the most concrete, yes, sir," Budenz replied.

During the small percentage of time that he was actually talking about me, Budenz put his emphasis on the years 1937 and 1943. The way in which he emphasized my connection with the Institute of Pacific Relations indicated that he had been prompted not so much by recollections of his own years in the Communist Party as by recent conferences with the China Lobby. Moreover, he had done his homework in a hurry. He did not seem to know that in the year 1943, when I was a Deputy Director of the Office of War Information and lived in San Francisco, I had had nothing whatever to do with the publications of the Institute of Pacific Relations. Nor did he seem to know that in 1936 and 1937 I had spent some of the time in Europe and most of the time in China, with a total of not more than about three months in America, so that I was in a very poor position to "organize" American writers.

While he was talking about these years my mind flashed back to our happy life in Peking — and afterwards Eleanor told me that hers had too. In those carefree years we had had little interest in politics. We danced at the French hotels and rode horseback and spent long week ends at temples in the Western Hills. Our house had been a sort of headquarters for Mongols coming down from Mongolia to Peking. "Politics" had for me meant chiefly the relations between Mongols, Chinese and Japanese. Of the party politics of all three peoples I knew little. We also had many friends in the American Embassy and other embassies, among the American and European scholars and research workers in Peking, and among Chinese scholars. We even had Japanese friends. The only connections we absolutely did not have were Communist connections. It was not until the early summer of 1937 that I had made a brief trip up to the Chinese Communist territory in Northwest China, and then I had stayed only four days. Indeed, when we came back to America at the end of 1937, if I had had to pass an examination on my qualifications as an expert on China, I would have been forced to admit that my weakest qualification was my knowledge of Communist theory and the ideology, political program, and organization of the Chinese Communists who were to become so important in the next few years. The one thing I did know for sure, after talking with a few of the Chinese Communist leaders on that one trip, was that they were copper-riveted, brass-bottomed Communists and not "just agrarian reformers."

No one brought out, in a way that would have made a simple and direct newspaper story, the fact that his accusations against me were hearsay that would not have stood up in a court of law; thus he was taking advantage of the legal immunity of appearing before a Senatorial Committee, not to establish facts but to make personal headlines. This was revealed only indirectly, when after his hearing he appeared on a television program and refused to repeat, under conditions that would have laid him open to a suit for libel, the things that he had said under immunity. "Budenz Backs Off Television," was the way one newspaper headed its story.

From my point of view as a man unjustly accused, the questioning of Budenz was unsatisfactory. It is a defect of the Senatorial Committee method of procedure, as compared with procedure in a court of law, that direct cross-examination is not allowed. In consultation with my lawyers, I could pass up questions to the Committee, but the members of the Committee, and Edward P. Morgan, the head of their legal staff, could ask these questions or not ask them as they saw fit. Most of our questions were not asked. All three of my lawyers were outspoken about their frustration. They said that if they had been able to cross-examine him in a court of law, they could have torn to pieces the thin case he had tried to build up against me. Under the Committee procedure, however, legal precision was almost entirely disregarded in favor of political tight-rope walking. It is a little incongruous to think of a sacred cow being handled with kid gloves, but that was the kind of handling that Budenz got. Except for questions by Senator Green and one or two questions from Senator Tydings and Senator Lodge, it was clear that the senators were afraid of tangling with a man with Budenz's politically influential backing.

This hesitant questioning failed to make clear enough the contrast between the big bang that had been expected from Budenz and the smoke without fire that was all that he could produce. To give reporters a chance to make the contrast clearer, I held a press conference the next day. This was my first experience of a Washington press conference, which I knew would be attended by the most sophisticated reporters in America — people accustomed to thinking every day of their lives in a double pattern of the political news that is printed and the political "inside dope" that isn't printed. So when I waited for questions from the men and women who packed Paul Porter's big office, I knew that the real test would be in the attitude of the reporters. Their questions soon showed that Budenz had flopped and that there was no "hot Washington tip" of revelations still to come. I could therefore take my time in working on the detailed refutation which I prepared for my second appearance before the Committee and which is summarized in Chapter VI. The most interested questions, in fact, were about the China Lobby, while one reporter's questions pointed up the fact that it must have been a colleague of mine at the Johns Hopkins who had been the source of the attempts to give a sinister twist to my visit to Alaska and to connect me with the Amerasia case.

At the end of the day the political nature of the hearing flared up in the open. The Republicans wanted to adjourn, so that the newspapers next day would be monopolized by Budenz. Abe Fortas, on my behalf, fought hard to get General Thorpe on the stand. Finally we got him on, and in his blunt and soldierly way he read his statement:

Any statements or expressions of opinion made by me at this hearing in no way reflect the opinions or policies of the Department of the Army and reflect only my own opinion.

I have spent something more than half my thirty-two years of army service doing intelligence work, the major portion in the Pacific Ocean and the Far East. I have done intelligence work in Hawaii, the countries of southeast Asia, Japan, Netherlands Indies, and the Philippines. During the war, I was chief of counter-intelligence and civil intelligence on the staff of General Douglas MacArthur. My last assignment prior to retiring in December was as military attaché at the American Embassy in Bangkok, Siam.

At this point I believe I should state I am not in possession of any files connected with my work, as they are, of course, in possession of the Department of the Army and consequently are not available to me, which I regard as quite proper. I do believe, however, it is entirely proper for me to express my strong conviction, based on careful examination, that Owen Lattimore is a loyal American citizen and is in no way an agent of the Communist Party nor of the USSR.

I have had three occasions to look into Owen Lattimore's conduct and loyalty. First, in the early '30's when I was examining the affairs of the Institute of Pacific Relations. Second, when he visited our theater of operations in 1944 and in 1946. Finally my last look at Dr. Lattimore was in 1947 while in charge of procuring Russian linguists for the Army.

To review these three instances, I should like first to mention the Institute of Pacific Relations. It is my personal belief that this organization contains within its membership highly respectable citizens interested in the Pacific basin and the furthering of peace in that part of the world. It also has associated with it educators interested in using its facilities in their education work. Finally it has, as have apparently all such organizations, the usual collection of intellectual panhandlers and screwballs. From my limited examination in recent years, I doubt the value of these latter characters to any intelligence-seeking organization.

As an intelligence officer of some years' experience, it is my belief that there is no information available to any foreign government through the Institute of Pacific Relations that can not be better had through the Government Printing Office, the Coast and Geodetic Survey or going and making a personal examination. In a country as free of access as this, there are practically no places denied foreign visitors other than a very few technical plants. I believe the Institute of Pacific Relations could profitably part with some of their people, but I doubt the capacity of such people to do any serious harm to the United States should they be so inclined.

To return to Dr. Lattimore, in examining the statements of the protagonists of Nationalist China on Dr. Lattimore, I have never, in my experience as an intelligence officer, heard a man so frequently referred to as a "Communist" with so little basis in fact. It is my belief based on careful examination that through the past ten years Dr. Lattimore's opinions on China have been the primary basis for this accusation of disloyalty.

It should be borne in mind that there are no neutral views on China. Interested persons are for the most part emotional and positive to an extreme degree. Repeatedly I found people willing to call Lattimore a Communist and then be unable to offer anything more in substantiation than the belief that his opinions on China were pleasing to the Communists. When I had finished looking into this man's loyalty, I found I had nothing but hearsay evidence, much of it obviously vindictive in character. There is no question in my mind that Dr. Lattimore has aroused a vigorous antipathy toward himself among the friends of the Chinese Nationalist cause.

As for Dr. Lattimore's ability to act as a "spy" for a foreign government, unless he has had access to top secret information of which I am not aware, regardless of his desires, I rate his capacity for such action so small as to be of no value.

Based on my belief that Dr. Lattimore is and has always

been a loyal citizen, during the early days of our occupation of Japan I asked and received his assistance in dealing with matters pertaining to the USSR of a confidential nature. His assistance was of material value. When in 1947 I again sought his assistance in acquiring and training Russian linguists, he again gave valuable aid.

For me to say I know the innermost thoughts or all the secret acts of Owen Lattimore would be absurd. I can only say that were I called on to commit my personal safety and that of my command on information by Dr. Lattimore, I would do so with confidence that he would always act as a loyal American citizen.

Following this testimony, he was questioned with a roughness that was in startling contrast with the deferential way in which Budenz had been handled. The questioning, however, strengthened the General's testimony. It brought out, for instance, the fact that when I had visited General MacArthur's theater in 1944, and when I had been in occupied Japan in 1945–46, there was "very close" co-operation between the F.B.I. and the military investigative service headed by General Thorpe. He was not dependent solely on locally available information when he cleared me.

He also emphasized that when I gave him advice when I was in Japan it was good advice; that in my aid to him he had no occasion to question my loyalty; and that I showed no partisanship for any country other than the United States. Finally, when Senator Green asked him what was his purpose in asking to be heard as a witness, he said: "Sir, I am here because I am greatly concerned about cutting off our sources of supply. I have stated my belief in regard to Dr. Lattimore, and no one else, and I am concerned that people who handle Communist documents, people who are seen with them, if they are accused of Communism when they in my opinion are not, it is going to cut off what little bit we have left in the way of information."

After the questioning of General Thorpe, Abe wanted to get into the record the affidavit from Bella Dodd.

Again the Republicans put up a fight to prevent this from being done in time to be quoted in the next day's newspapers. This time they were successful — but only as far as the official record was concerned. Knowing that the battle was being fought largely in the newspapers and that we had to be tough about it, my lawyers released the affidavit to the press:

STATE OF NEW YORK
COUNTY OF NEW YORK

BELLA V. DODD, being duly sworn deposes and says:

As a member of the Communist Party I was elected to its national Committee in 1944. The National Committee is the chief policy making body of the Party. I served on the National Committee for four years from 1944 to 1948. During that period I also served on the New York State Committee of the Party. I was a member of the New York State Board which is the highest executive Committee in the State, and I served as the Party legislative representative for New York.

During this time I frequently conferred with National Party leaders on political, labor and legislative questions. I attended many conferences on international affairs including discussions on the Far East and China.

Particularly in my position as legislative representative it was my duty to study, analyze, and report on developments on the political and legislative front in Washington and in Albany. I was therefore in a position to know public figures who were friendly to or useful in promoting our legislative and political program.

I was expelled from the Communist Party in June, 1949 after charges had been preferred against me on account of my opposition to certain policies of the Party.

I am not now a member of the Communist Party and have no ties with it whatsoever.

I knew Louis Budenz who was the managing editor of the *Daily Worker*. He first became a member of the National Committee in 1944 at the same time I was elected to that body. He served as a member for about one year. During this time his primary responsibility was to get out the *Daily Worker*, under the direction of the National Board.

I have never met Owen Lattimore. I never heard of him until the present controversy. In all my association with the Communist Party I never heard his name mentioned by Party leaders or friends of the Party as a Party member or a friend of the Party.

I am making this affidavit reluctantly because since my expulsion from the Party I have been trying to live a private life and to devote myself exclusively to the practice of law. I break my silence only because a grave injustice may be done by mistaken persons whose tactics may well be injurious to our national welfare.

/ s /　Bella V. Dodd

(SEAL)
Sworn to before me
this *19th* day of *April.*

/ s /　Sidney Friedman

We went home that night bone-tired from the nervous strain of the day but we were cheered during the next two days to find that there was a wide and prompt realization both in the press and among the public that the Budenz charges would not hold water. Despite his indirect and unsubstantiated charges against me, Budenz might have smeared me successfully had it not been for the fact that by now I had had a chance to put my record clearly before the public. A large part of the press and radio had already pointed out the basic honesty and soundness of my case; and McCarthy had strengthened my case by publicly weaseling on his declarations that he was not afraid to repeat, off the floor of the Senate, the charges that he had made under immunity. It was conspicuously obvious that the Budenz testimony did not provide him with the courage that had so long been lacking.

During these days we received many letters and newspaper editorial clippings about Budenz's assertion that there are hidden Communists who act as if they are anti-Communists. They all pointed out that by this logic Budenz's actions, talk, and position as professor in a Catholic university would make it quite believable that he is himself a hidden Communist.

The next development was the "Battle of the Ex-Communists." This battle had to be fought out before I came forward to make another public statement, because McCarthy's tactics were obviously to wear me down by raising one accusation, having me make an appearance in rebuttal, then raising another accusation, having me appear again, and so on without end. Senator Tydings, however, made a very fair ruling: all accusations against me had to be heard first, and after that I was to have the right to appear and deal with all of them at once.

Since McCarthy had made his charges against me on the Senate floor, where they had received the maximum amount of publicity, my lawyers had requested the Committee that all hearings which had to do with my case should be public hearings, and Senator Tydings had agreed to this. At the close of the Budenz hearing, however, he announced a closed executive session for the following morning at which Budenz was to make further accusations, some of them presumably affecting me and some affecting other people. I was told that I could attend this hearing, together with legal counsel, as long as Budenz had anything to say about me. McCarthy was to have the right to be there the same length of time.

On the morning of April 21 I went to the small Committee room together with Paul Porter. Budenz came in, and then McCarthy. Then a wrangle began among the members of the Committee. Senator Lodge had on previous occasions repeatedly called the whole system of committee hearings on loyalty investigations a public circus and had urged a totally different procedure under which all hearings would be private. I entirely agreed with him in theory, in cases in which public accusations had not been made, but it seemed to me completely unjust to insist on changing the procedure in the middle of my case, in a way which would give McCarthy the completest possible immunity. It would have meant accusation by headline and defense in silence. Or worse than silence, because any babe in the woods, let alone a Republican politician, knew that as long as McCarthy had pipelines into the Committee, executive sessions could not be kept secret and that whatever information leaked would be distorted.

Hickenlooper backed up Lodge's arguments, but not for Lodge's reasons. It was obvious that Hickenlooper wanted to get me excluded from this meeting so that I would not be able to hear what Budenz had to say. Whatever was said in nominal secrecy would then leak to McCarthy, and McCarthy would exploit it by taking advantage of the immunity of the Senate floor. This was exactly what happened. There was a leak, though not relating to me, and McCarthy did exploit it on the Senate floor — but evidently with such an outrageous distortion that it was too much for the stomachs even of the Republican members of the Subcommittee. A spokesman of the Subcommittee — not just the Democratic members, but the full Subcommittee — publicly disowned what McCarthy had said.

As far as this one meeting was concerned Lodge and Hickenlooper won out. Senator Tydings, with only one other Democrat present, so that he did not have a clear majority, leaned over backward to avoid any possible accusation of making too strong a use of his authority as Chairman. Paul Porter and I were asked to withdraw. McCarthy remained, temporarily, to put up a fight for the "Senatorial courtesy" of being allowed to sit in on the meeting, though not a member of the Senate Committee on Foreign Relations. As I left the room, I heard him say cockily that he ought to be allowed to remain because he "knew much more about cross-examining" than anyone else there — which must have been galling to the older and more experienced members of the Subcommittee, with many more years of legal experience than he. Eventually, however, he was not allowed to stay.

The next public hearings were those of Dr. Bella Dodd, Earl Browder, Frederick V. Field and Freda Utley. I attended the hearings for Dr. Dodd and Freda Utley, but not those for Browder and Field. I think their testimony showed that there is a good deal of diversity and even confusion in the ranks of the Communists, and certainly among the ex-Communists.

Obviously there is a conspiratorial layer sandwiched in somewhere in the Party. It seems to be typical of Budenz's obsession with sensationalism that he tries to make out that there is nothing in the sandwich except the conspiratorial layer. The evidence of the other ex-Communists does not bear this out. Dr. Bella Dodd, for instance, does not seem to me to be the kind of person who could ever have been a conspirator. She impresses me rather as the kind of person with whom I would disagree completely in a political argument, without feeling that I had any reason to suspect her of political dishonesty or lack of moral integrity.

Earl Browder strikes me, from his testimony and the descriptions of him at the hearing, as a man who is stubbornly convinced of the fundamental rightness of his own opinion. Stubbornness, however, is not the same thing as dishonesty, and even fanatic stubbornness is not the same thing as conspiracy.

Frederick V. Field is a man of yet another type, very different from any of the others. He is frequently and publicly listed as a Communist, though as far as I know he has neither admitted nor denied Party membership. He strikes me as an individualist who has gone over so far to the left that there is nobody else there except the Communists. Years ago, when I knew him in the Institute of Pacific Relations, he always seemed to be working for the best interests of the Institute. To the extent that I met him in committee meetings or dealt with him administratively, I never knew him to try tricking his associates into upholding or promoting the Communist line. And I ought to add that I never saw a situation in the Institute of Pacific Relations in which he would not have been promptly squelched if he had tried it.

The most childish absurdity in the Kohlberg-McCarthy-Budenz charges against me is the suggestion that my ideas about China and the Far East could in any way have been dominated or controlled by Mr. Field. My opinions on Asia, being founded on years of travel and independent study, have always been independently evolved. I am therefore not being high and mighty when I point out that when I used to talk about the history and problems of China and the Far East with Mr. Field — who incidentally is a good deal younger than I am — I was on the telling end and he was on the listening end. The perfectly natural relationship was for him to consult me on both facts and opinions.

It seemed to me that the members of the Subcommittee got themselves all mixed up because each of them, in his own way, tried to find some kind of simple formula that would enable him to classify all of these very different people as uniform, interchangeable parts of a standardized machine, when obviously they weren't. Certainly one thing stands out. Budenz, in his Communist days, must have been an extremely shifty, tricky, conspiratorial character. He not only admits this in his own book, but keeps rubbing his own nose in the degradation of the Communist chapter in his past. The others seemed to me to be, each in an individual and different way, opinionated and even stubborn, and hostile to the Committee that was questioning them, but sincere.

Dr. Dodd and Mr. Browder proved that there is no uniformity among ex-Communists. They obviously differed from each other and they even more obviously differed from Budenz. Both of them contradicted him not only on the question of any association between me and the Communists but on important details of Communist organization and the management of the *Daily Worker*, which Budenz at one time edited. Browder added that he considered me to be "profoundly anti-Communist."

Mr. Field had previously written to Abe Fortas that it was an "outright lie" to say that he had ever told Budenz that I was a member of the Communist Party or subject to Party discipline. He added that to the best of his knowledge he never discussed me "in any manner whatsoever with Mr. Budenz or in his presence," and that he "never told Budenz, or anyone else for that matter, that Lattimore was a person on whom the Communist Party could rely or that he was a person who could be useful to the Communist Party."

There was one amusing interlude in the long-drawn skirmish of the ex-Communists. This was the incident of the disappearing witness, John J. Huber. On the day that Bella Dodd testified, McCarthy was hard up for ammunition. So he went up to New York and brought back with him by plane two men who had formerly been connected with the F.B.I. One of them, named Lawrence E. Kerley, had joined a Hearst paper, the *New York Journal-American*, after leaving the F.B.I. The other, John J. Huber, had never been in the F.B.I. properly speaking, but had served it as an informer. These two men spent a morning in McCarthy's office and then left, supposedly to register at the Carlton Hotel.

When Kerley was called to the stand, it was apparently for the purpose of identifying Huber's connection with the F.B.I., by testifying that he was the man who had registered Huber's name with the F.B.I. Having given this testimony, however, he started to slip smoothly into hearsay testimony, saying that Huber had told him that he had seen me in 1946 at a party in the home of Frederick V. Field, in connection with a meeting of the Committee for a Democratic Far Eastern Policy — a group which is on the Attorney General's list as subversive. At this point he was interrupted. If this was to be Huber's testimony, Huber should now come forward and give it in person.

Huber's name was then called. He did not answer and did not come forward. There was a sensation. A five-minute recess was called. Someone went to the telephone to try to trace him. McCarthy, looking rather sick, slipped out of the room and disappeared, which looked as though he did not expect Huber to turn up. Among the hard-boiled newspapermen, the momentary sensation quickly turned into cynical amusement. They obviously thought that Huber was a phony, had got cold feet, and had disappeared rather than testify. In the next day or two there was a certain amount of excitement about Huber, but it was quickly obvious that he was not going to turn up and that nobody was going to try to find him. As a way of tapering off the excitement a story was put around by or on behalf of Huber. He was supposed to have turned up in New York and to have called various people on the telephone, explaining that he had "blacked out" in Washington, had turned up in New York, and was going to rest up. Nothing more happened.

This story shows how, in the hysteria of a witch-hunt, every possible consideration is extended to the ordinarily despised common informer. This special consideration can be carried to such excess that all is forgiven and forgotten even if, at the last moment, his courage fails him and he runs out on his assignment. Willingness to have started out to join the witch-hunt is the saving grace. By the same token, willingness to start out to oppose the witch-hunt would expose a man to suspicion. It is interesting to speculate on what would have happened if, for instance, I had announced that I would produce a key witness, and the witness had then vanished. My guess is that bloodhounds would have been laid on the trail and neither press nor police would have rested until the missing witness had been run to earth. In the meantime, McCarthy would have made one speech after another, charging me with attempts to bribe or to intimidate an unwilling witness to commit perjury.

In the case of Huber the basic facts are that as recently as September 8, September 9, and October 28, 1949, both Kerley and Huber had appeared as witnesses in public hearings before the McCarran Subcommittee of the Senate Judiciary Committee to testify on "Communist activities among aliens and national groups." Huber's testimony runs to more than one hundred printed pages, in which hundreds of names are mentioned. The index to this testimony has three references to Communist policy on China, eight references to Frederick V. Field, and fourteen references to the Committee for a Democratic Far Eastern Policy — but in all the hundreds of names that are mentioned, mine is missing. In addition, Huber submitted a thousand-page diary that he kept between the years 1938 and 1947 — and my name was not in this diary.

At this time Huber was working as an informer for the F.B.I. If in his routine reports he had mentioned my name as attending a meeting at Field's house, the charge could hardly have been omitted from the summary of my F.B.I. file shown to the Subcommittee, on the strength of which Senator Tydings had announced, after my first hearing, that I was absolutely in the clear.

Huber knew that members of the Committee had seen the summary of the F.B.I. files. If, after that, he had testified on oath that I had attended the alleged party, the Committee might have checked directly with the F.B.I. file and discovered a discrepancy that would expose him to the danger of a perjury charge.

It was after ten at night when this session was over. We went back to Abe Fortas's house and I issued a statement to the press making it clear that I had never been at a meeting in Field's house and had never belonged to the Committee for a Democratic Far Eastern Policy.

McCarthy still had one more witness, though the rumor was going around Washington that he was hesitating to put her on because he was afraid that she would prove to be a witness more damaging to him than to me. This was Freda Utley, once a member of the British Communist

Party, once married to a Russian — at which time she lived in Moscow for some years and worked for the Soviet Government — once an active propagandist for America First and appeasement of Hitler, and more recently an active member of the China Lobby, closely associated with Kohlberg.

I had met Freda Utley in Moscow in 1936. A couple of weeks later, when I was crossing from Holland to England, I was surprised to find her on the same boat. She was terribly upset and told me that her husband had been arrested in Moscow by the secret police. I had felt the same shock and pity for her that any American would have felt; helped her and her child on the boat, and when we got to England, helped her in landing and in getting on the train. Later that year, my wife and I spent several months in London. Here we again saw Freda Utley several times. At her house, I met a number of ex-Communists, all of them very bitter and cynical.

From England my wife and I returned to China, where we stayed until the end of 1937. Then we came back to America and in the fall of 1938 I took up my new post at the Page School of International Relations at the Johns Hopkins. In 1939, Freda Utley came to America and came straight to Baltimore to stay with us. She had been in China, and was now anxious to write and lecture in America. We gave her hospitality for several weeks, and I did everything I could to get her lecture engagements and opportunities to write.

By 1940, however, we were seeing much less of her, because she was becoming more and more isolationist, was associating herself with the America First propaganda, and was in favor of appeasing Hitler, while Eleanor and I, though far from enthusiastic about the Chamberlain government in Britain or the situation in France, saw no sense whatever in attempting to appease Hitler. Of course we sympathized with her more and more despairing hope of helping her husband, and she continuously sought to enlist my help, but there was not much that anyone could do about it, since after all he was neither American nor British but Russian. I did all I could, which was pitifully little, but she seemed convinced that I could have done more if I had wanted to. A psychiatrist could probably make more sense of it than I can, but it was almost as if, when she finally gave up all hope of ever seeing her husband again, she made me a symbol of her frustration and despair. At any rate, from that time on she became not only a passionate campaigner against Stalin, Russia, and the Russians, and an eloquent propagandist in favor of the appeasement of Nazi Germany, but also began to slander me among our friends in Baltimore. I then found in her something that I have since noticed in several other ex-Communists — it is not enough for you to be a non-Communist or an anti-Communist; if you are not anti-Communist in exactly the same way that they are, and for exactly the same reasons, then they are apt to call you a "Stalinist" — though I do not see how it is possible for a person who has never been a Communist to be anti-Communist in exactly the same way as an ex-Communist.

Freda Utley launched into her attack on me not like an American trying to influence a group of Senators whose minds worked along American political lines, but like a disillusioned intellectual in some dim, faraway Bloomsbury parlor, exchanging with other disappointed radicals a confused barrage of slogans learned by heart long ago, ideological quotations, and bits of old, turgid, but still bitter sectarian dispute. It had nothing to do with me. It was as if she were carrying on some civil war, some unforgotten quarrel with her old Marxist cronies, pawing over things I had written, to pounce on half a sentence here and part of a paragraph there to hurl, not really at me, but at them in an effort, meaningless to non-Marxists, to prove that somehow her ideology was more ideological than their ideology.

It was a perfect demonstration of why the doctrinaire mind, trained on Marxism, fails to convince the American mind. She had in front of her an enormous pile of papers in which she could never find what she wanted when she wanted it. The newspapermen soon got tired of it. The senators began to get impatient, too. They interrupted her more and more frequently. Senator Tydings pressed her over and over again for facts, not opinion — "what we want is F-A-C-T-S," said Senator Tydings. She was flustered, and the more flustered she got, the fewer the facts and the wider and more sweeping the opinions. She said, for example, that I "tried to influence Americans by quoting from people like Wendell Willkie," which must deserve some kind of a prize as one of the most irrelevant things ever said in an attempt to smear a man as a Communist.

When asked whether she agreed with McCarthy's charge that I was the "top Russian espionage agent," she drew an incredulous laugh by saying that I was something much more serious and important than that, and then went on to say that "all spies are expendable," and I was of "far too great value in influencing American opinion" on China for the Russians to have used me as an expendable spy. She then groped around for a phrase, and with the invincible English talent for getting all balled up on American slang, came up with one that caught the fancy of the press; she described me as a "Judas cow" whom the entire American people were dumbly following to slaughter. It struck me as the kind of reasoning that would turn up only among readers of ideological magazines, arguing among themselves in little, frustrated groups, about world-shaking events.

My thoughts turned to China, in which I have spent so many years. Here, in a land as vast as America itself, a population of four hundred fifty million has been shaken for forty years by political and economic convulsions. Famine, revolution, civil war, foreign invasion, and civil war again have swept the land. Millions of people have been starved to death or killed, millions of people have lost their homes and wandered into far provinces. The family system that used to strengthen the fabric of society has been disrupted. China has become one of the world's great problems; inside China the whole society heaves and twists with contributory problems. We are no longer in the nineteenth century, when small expeditionary forces of the great powers could march in and lay down the law. All the great powers of the world, including Russia as well as the United States, can no longer assert in China their theories of what China ought to be; all of them have to adjust themselves to the turbulent facts of China as it is. I can think of nothing more incredible and farfetched than the assertion, by a disillusioned Marxist, that this cumulation of the events of forty years, now reaching a thundering climax whose outcome we cannot foresee, and its impact on America, is all the handiwork of one professor of international relations in an American university.

Under questioning, it was brought out that Freda Utley, who professed to have made a profound study and analysis of my writings, could not show that I had ever followed the Party line even to the mild extent of calling the Chinese Communists "agrarian radicals," but that she herself had described them in phrases of that kind. In 1939, for example, she had said that "the Chinese Communists today neither proclaim nor follow a revolutionary policy fatal to the possessing classes or Chiang Kai-shek himself," and had said that they really ought to "call themselves Radicals in the English nineteenth-century meaning of the word."

Questioning also brought out the long record of her pro-Nazi writing, and the fact that, in a book published in 1949, she had made many allegations of Communist infiltration and domination of American postwar policy in Germany including — to give only one quotation — such assertions as "there are grounds for suspecting that Brigadier-General Telford Taylor, who as chief counsel for war crimes directed the Nuremberg trials after Justice Jackson's departure, was sympathetic to the Soviet Union." Here Freda Utley grew more flustered than ever. Having herself made an effort to cast suspicion on me by bits and patches of quotation, taken out of context, she now flung herself back in her chair and cried out plaintively that "if this is going to be an examination of my writings, I wish you would look at the whole book." I was hardly surprised when, after the hearing was adjourned, a stranger said to me as we were going out, "Freda Utley is the best witness you have had."

CHAPTER VI

IT WAS NOW MAY 2 — nearly a month after my first hearing. McCarthy's big gun, Budenz, had misfired. Huber and Freda Utley had provided only ludicrous anticlimaxes. It was my turn at last to review the whole grotesque, brutal, and long-sustained attempt at character-assassination.

Once more the Caucus Room was packed so tightly that there were people standing around the edges, against the wall. The batteries of newsreel cameras were there too, but I soon noticed an encouraging sign. Instead of the lights blazing and the cameras whirring all the time, they went on only occasionally. That meant, I thought, that the newsreels were not on tiptoe with expectation. The sensationalism of the charges against me had already been somewhat deflated.

Because it had been so long since my first hearing, I began by reminding the Committee of the original charges that Senator McCarthy had made against me from a foxhole of immunity on the Senate floor, and then went on:

Since that time he has obviously been engaged in a frenzied effort to prove them, or at least to make them appear plausible. He has been assisted by a staff paid to beat the bushes for something, anything that will take the Senator off the spot.

First, the Senator has said that I am "the top Russian espionage agent in the United States." Not even the Senator's own procured witnesses were willing to support this.

Second, the Senator said that I am "*one* of the top Communist agents in this country." None of the witnesses even attempted to support this.

Third, the Senator said that I am "a Soviet agent." No evidence supports this.

A reading of the record fails to show that any witness directly charged that I was a member of the Communist Party.

I have never been an official of the Department of State or the "architect" of its Far Eastern policy. I and I alone am responsible for what I have written and done. I hope that it is clear beyond question that you are here investigating a private American citizen: a university professor, a journalist, an author and lecturer. You are investigating a man who has spent his life in business activities and studies in the Far East, who has written and lectured extensively concerning his specialty, and who has strong views concerning the past, present and future of that area, which he has freely and publicly expressed.

Senator McCarthy, however, has chosen to stake the validity of his charges against the State Department and to stake his own reputation on his accusations against me. I am glad to accept the role in which he has cast me, and by proving that his charges are false and malicious to silence the Senator once and for all — or to show again that his word is worthless. I ask only that this Committee render its verdict in clear-cut terms, so that the Senator can then be plainly advised that he has been caught out in his fraud and deceit; that he has lost his test case; and that he should henceforth confine himself to other activities than those of a destructive critic of the State Department and a despoiler of the character of good American citizens. The Senator, to use his own term, is clearly a bad policy risk.

Now, gentlemen, I of course do not enjoy being vilified by anybody: even by the motley crew of crackpots, professional informers, hysterics and ex-Communists who, McCarthy would have you believe, represent sound Americanism. But on the other hand, I do not like to appear to rely upon the testimony of others to establish my own good character. My life and works speak for themselves. Unlike McCarthy I have never been charged with a violation of the laws of the United States or of the ethics of my profession. I have never been accused, as McCarthy has been, of income-tax evasion, of the destruction of records that were in my official custody, or of improperly using an official position for the purpose of advancing my own fortunes, political or otherwise.

Unlike Budenz and Utley, I have never been a member of the Communist Party, or subscribed to a conspiracy to overthrow and subvert established governments. Unlike Budenz, I have never engaged in a conspiracy to commit murder or espionage.

I have examined the Attorney General's consolidated list of subversive organizations and to the best of my knowledge and belief I have never been a member of any of them.

I recognize, however, that so long as a reckless and irresponsible man like Joseph McCarthy is in a position to abuse the privileges of the United States Congress, the quality of a man's life and activities, however impeccable, does not protect him from vile assault. Accordingly, I am forced to take your time to analyze and answer in detail the so-called evidence that this man McCarthy has presented in his effort to blacken the name of an American citizen.

Now as to Freda Utley.

This witness stated that she had no evidence that I was at

any time a member of the Communist Party; she stated that she had no knowledge or information that I was an espionage agent, and said that she thought that Senator McCarthy was "wrong" on that point.

To the extent that any evidence in support of McCarthy's charges has been submitted, then, it is to be found only in the testimony of the witness Budenz. I hope that the members of this Committee will find time in their crowded schedules to *read* this testimony. I also hope that the members of the press will read it. Disassociated from the fervor of Budenz's fanaticism — incidentally, he must have been a very zealous Communist — the statements that he made unmistakably lead to two conclusions: First, Budenz did not even pretend to have any factual information about me or my works; second, the screen of lies behind which he disguised his lack of information is very thin, indeed.

I then summarized the Budenz testimony — some of which has already been discussed in Chapter V.

At one point in his testimony Budenz had admitted that he had "never seen any vestige" of my Communist Party membership. What he claimed was that he had been told by Earl Browder and F. V. Field — both of whom denied it — that I was "responsible for the placing of a number of Communist writers" in organs of the Institute of Pacific Relations. This was supposed to have happened in 1937, although I was out of the United States for the whole of this year, returning only at the very end of December. When asked to identify me directly as a Communist, he slid off into general discussion of the different kinds of Communists, but never stated on his own responsibility that I was or am any one of the fifty-seven varieties.

When asked by Senator Lodge, as I have already described, to give a specific instance when an order or an instruction was given to me and carried out, he lamely alleged that "according to reports" I had "mobilized writers," but even then tried to straddle by saying that he "did not hear the detailed report." This, according to his own admission, was "the most concrete" illustration he could give.

Budenz alleged that at a Communist meeting in 1943, I, through *F. V. Field*, "had received word from the apparatus that there was to be a change of line on Chiang Kai-shek." Under cross-examination he casually changed his story, although with rather obvious misgivings. He said: "Mr. Field reported, as I understand it, that he had seen Mr. Lattimore . . . and that *Mr. Lattimore* had said that the apparatus had reported that there was a change of attitude . . . that we were going to be more hostile to Chiang Kai-shek," and that this new line was to be carried out in an article in one of the publications of the Institute of Pacific Relations. Whether in the form that I told Mr. Field or that he told me, this yarn was as fantastic as it was malignant. In 1943 I was an employee of the Office of War Information, and had no connection with any publication of the Institute of Pacific Relations. I did not at that time — or at any time — know about changes in the Communist Party line from anybody. Actually it was in 1943 that I was most vigorous in my support and praise of Chiang Kai-shek. As I said in my statement:

Indeed, the fact of the matter is that for many years after the change in the Party line I was still vigorously supporting

Chiang Kai-shek. I shall go into this later in my statement. It will suffice for the moment to say that I have never, in any of my writings, in any speech or in any conversation, criticized the person of Generalissimo Chiang Kai-shek. I have criticized his policies. I have criticized his advisers. In memoranda and discussions with him and in published works, I have urged him to change his course. But I have never and shall never change my view of him as a great man of his time, with all his good qualities and weaknesses. Late in 1943 after the American Communists began their vicious, personal assault on him, I said he was a "world statesman of real genius." In *Solution in Asia*, published in 1945, I said on page 83, "Chiang never became a dictator or a fascist."

At about this same time, Chiang was being referred to in the *Daily Worker*, of which Budenz was Managing Editor, as a dictator and a member of Shanghai's Green Gang. (*Daily Worker*, September 12, 1945, September 11, 1945.)

The third allegation by Budenz was that in 1944 a high-up Communist named Jack Stachel advised him "to consider Owen Lattimore as a Communist," which according to Budenz meant "to treat as authoritative" anything that I might say or advise. Needless to say, I have never known Mr. Stachel and when Budenz mentioned him his name meant nothing to me.

Presumably Budenz meant to convey the impression that in his job as Managing Editor of the *Daily Worker* he was to treat as authoritative anything I might say or advise. If so, Budenz certainly did not obey instructions, because in his obsequious editing of the *Daily Worker* under the orders of his Communist superiors he certainly did not reflect my opinions and attitudes on the Chinese situation. It was in

1944 that Eleanor and I, as joint authors, published *The Making of Modern China*, later republished as *China, A Short History*, which led to my being called a "libeler of the Chinese Communist Party" by one of the leading Russian historical journals. Then and later I urged that the way to stop the spread of Communism in China was to support democratic reforms; and then and later I urged that American policy promote the creation of conditions under which private capitalism might flourish in the Far East. I particularly drew attention to the importance of the small but modern-minded capitalist class in China and other countries in Asia. I doubt if these "authoritative" ideas of mine can be found in the *Daily Worker* as edited by Budenz — or since Budenz.

The prize cloak-and-dagger Budenz story was one about supersecret documents on onionskin paper circulated among Communist officials. He claimed that he was told that I was referred to in some of these documents under the cabalistic code reference of L or XL; but he also claimed that the documents were so secret that, after being read, they had to be put down the drain immediately — which is where the whole preposterous yarn belongs.

The final attempt by Budenz to implicate me in his own lurid world of conspiracy was the allegation — again in his favorite form of hearsay — that he had been told by Jack Stachel that I had been of assistance to some of the defendants in the *Amerasia* case. I had no connection with the *Amerasia* case, as I had said in my first statement. In my statement, I summed up the Budenz testimony as "pure moonshine, or rather impure hogwash, the product of a twisted and malignant personality."

With regard to the general credibility of Budenz there were also important points to be made.

1. After leaving the Communist Party in 1945 Budenz had testified before about a dozen governmental agencies and courts. At no time in all these years did he even mention me.

2. He himself emphasized the endless hours he had spent with the F.B.I., informing them about the Communist Party. He never mentioned me, by his own admission, until some time in March, 1950, after I had been accused by McCarthy and after the Committee had been shown a summary of my F.B.I. file. He complained unconvincingly that he had not had time to denounce me; but if I had been a sinister character he could at least have told the F.B.I. that I required investigation. That would have taken about thirty seconds of his time.

The plain fact of the matter seems to be that Budenz is engaged in a transparent hocus-pocus. Whenever anybody is conspicuously accused of Communist affiliations, Budenz hops on the band wagon and repeats the charges, garnished with more or less impressive references to Jack Stachel and others he considers to be Communist big shots. I suspect that he may invoke these names because he believes that Communists will refuse to testify in rebuttal. But he guards himself against even this contingency by saying that even if they do testify against what he says, they cannot be believed — about as ingenious a booby trap as has ever been devised.

3. In March, 1949, Budenz published an article in *Collier's* magazine aimed squarely at the importance of China and alleged Communist influence on our China policy. In

this article he denounced a number of people, but all he said about me was that I was an adherent of the Chinese agrarian-reformer theory — which was not true. After a conference with the associate editor of the magazine, he took out even this reference. The transcript of this conference, which I had submitted to the Committee and put into the record, shows the following questions by the associate editor of *Collier's* and answers by Budenz:

QUESTION: You have done one thing here that I think is not good. By inference you implied that Joe Barnes and Lattimore are not Communists exactly but are fellow travelers . . .

ANSWER (by Budenz): I think probably what we ought to do is to leave out those names entirely. Perhaps we can re-phrase it some way. I said it merely to show that they would add meat to what I was saying.

This interview went on:

QUESTION: You're not saying that they acted as Communist agents in any way?
ANSWER: No.
QUESTION: That ought to be quite clear.
ANSWER: Oh yes.

The clear and simple explanation of this interview is that at the time, just a year previously, it had not occurred even to this professional denouncer and informer, Budenz, that there was any basis whatever for accusing me of being a fellow traveler or a Communist agent.

He tried to wriggle out of this by saying that he was afraid of libel suits — but he had not said that to the *Collier's* editor who would, of course, on behalf of the magazine, also have felt the need to guard against libel. Budenz hedged, uncomfortably, by saying that the questions and attitude of the associate editor were "peculiar" — an innuendo against the motives of the associate editor.

4. The fact was also brought out that Budenz had in the hands of his publishers a book containing an extensive discussion of China and the Far East. In this book a lot of people were damagingly mentioned — but my name was added only after the book (*Men Without Faces*, Harper and Brothers, 1950) had reached the galley proof stage and after McCarthy made his charges against me. The comparison between galley proof and published text is an interesting illustration of the slapdash methods of a smear artist:

In the galleys, sent out to book reviewers before publication, the following passage appeared on galley proof 91A: ". . . John S. Service, now American ambassador to Indo-China. A champion of the Chinese Communists and an adviser to General Stilwell in China, he was one of those who urged a coalition between the Chinese Nationalists and the Communists; he also served as adviser to Henry Wallace and General George Marshall on Chinese affairs. . . ."

Published text, p. 265: ". . . John S. Service, now American consul in Calcutta. A champion of the Chinese Communists and an adviser to General Stilwell in China, he was one of those who urged a coalition between the Chinese Nationalists and the Communists; he also served with Owen J. Lattimore as adviser to Vice-President Henry Wallace and to our government on Chinese affairs. . . ."

In the amended passage, the ridiculous mistake about "ambassador to Indo-China" has been taken out, and Budenz had also apparently discovered — or someone had discovered for him — that Mr. Service did not serve as adviser to General Marshall, but the following misstatements or errors of fact remain:

Mr. Service was never a "champion" of the Chinese Communists. He was one of the able young State Department men who, in the course of duty, discovered and accurately reported that the Chinese Communists were of growing military and political importance, and had considerable popular backing.

My name is incorrectly given — there is no "J" or other middle initial in my name.

Mr. Service never served with me "as adviser to Vice-President Henry Wallace and to our government on Chinese affairs."

Specifically, the statement that I myself ever served as an "adviser" to our government on Chinese affairs is false, as could easily have been checked by a letter or telephone call to the State Department.

In my statement I referred to the fact that Budenz, in the four or five years since he had left the Communist Party, had not until a few weeks previously accused or denounced me as a fellow traveler, a Communist Party member, a person subject to Communist discipline, or a Soviet agent. He had not mentioned me to the F.B.I. or in any of his testimony before committees of the House and Senate, or in his appearances before Government agencies, grand juries, or courts. I continued:

This kind of skulduggery would be bad enough if it involved only one man and one crisis. But now this person has the consummate effrontery to say that he is preparing lists of hundreds of persons from the radio, press, Hollywood, government and other walks of life; and that he will denounce these people, presumably with the same kind of despicable charges that he has made against me. Why hasn't this professional informer named the persons that he accuses long before this time?

I cannot believe that the American government or the American people will permit this man to convert his thriving retail business into a wholesale enterprise and to continue to abuse the processes and immunities of committees of Congress. He should be forced to turn over the names, spurious or otherwise, of his victims to the F.B.I. where they may be held in confidence and subjected to the orderly and thorough processes of that agency.

We cannot allow this man to run wild any longer.

I then pointed out that Budenz had described himself as being, for ten long years, a member of a conspiracy to overthrow the government of the United States. According to his own description, he had been neither a dupe nor a visionary. In his book, *This Is My Story*, he writes that only a few months after he joined the Communist Party, he became convinced that the American Communist Party was under the immediate, personal control of a Russian state agent. He says, "My American conscience revolted at the idea" (page 136). Nevertheless, for more than nine years thereafter, he remained a loyal and effective Party official.

All of this evidence, I pointed out, showed that when Budenz entered the Communist Party he was not a young idealist. He was a hardened man of forty-four years. When he left the Party, he was a man of fifty-four, fully indoctrinated, according to his own account, in conspiratorial techniques.

He had also testified under oath that in 1943 on instructions of a Soviet representative he "established connections which involved espionage on American military agents," and that prior to that he had worked for three years with the Soviet secret police to plot the assassination of Leon Trotsky. To document his testimony, I made available to the Committee copy of the transcript of *In the Matter of Reinecke*, August 6, 1948, page 31. I have of course no way of knowing whether his testimony was true or not. The point is that this was the way, true or false, in which he testified about his own past.

I also submitted, in a sealed envelope, Budenz's sworn testimony, under cross-examination, in the official transcript of the deportation proceedings entitled: *In the Matter of Desideriu Hammer, alias John Santo, Respondent in Deportation Proceedings File No. A-6002664.* Beginning at page 143 of this transcript Budenz admitted that even before he joined the Communist Party he engaged in certain personal activities which, to say the least, are offensive to accepted standards of decent and conventional behavior. Beginning on page 170 of the transcript, he refused to reply to questions relating to his personal behavior, on the ground that his answers might incriminate him. These questions all concerned Budenz's activities *before* he became a member of the Communist Party. These indications of Budenz's sordid personal life were referred to by Senator Denis Chavez of New Mexico in a speech in the Senate on May 12. Chavez, himself a Catholic, scathingly denounced Budenz and stated his own belief that Budenz was still a Communist.

I then summed up what strongly impressed me as significant in Budenz's career after he left the Communists in 1945:

Since that time, he has been engaged in commercial exploitation of his own sordid past, resorting to methods which, in my opinion, are a menace to our society. I respectfully draw your attention, Senators, to the fact that when a man like Budenz becomes a renegade from a secret party or conspiracy such as he has himself described the American Communist Party to be, he automatically drops an iron curtain behind himself. From that moment on, he has no new sources of information. His sources are all in the past.

Now consider the kind of career that Budenz has been following for five years. He has made himself a sensational author and lecturer by exploiting his own past. But the past is the past, and he must be haunted by the fact that his tales of skulduggery and conspiracy may grow stale through sheer repetition. Already there have been new sensational revelations by government agents who have successfully infiltrated the Communist Party, and who have appeared at trials to give their testimony.

The pressure on Budenz is obvious. When a new sensation breaks out in the press and a man is accused — even if the accusation is false — what is the temptation that is dangled before him? It is the easiest thing in the world for his own memory to be convenient and obliging. He can then rush up and say "I remember him too!" — and thus revive his reputation as the peerless informant.

Whether there are other pressures and inducements operating upon Budenz, I do not know. This alone would be adequate for a man whose character is so plainly exhibited in his life and works. His basic representation, I submit, is completely incredible: that is, that while Managing Editor of the *Daily Worker*, he was given from time to time a list of a thousand names, and that he draws upon a prodigious memory now, five years later, and for the first time produces my name and a great deal of circumstantial detail.

I have already pointed out that his story is, on its face, at variance with the facts of record about me. You have heard other witnesses contradict him on specific and general parts of his statement. You have yourselves developed the fact, which I have summarized, that Budenz never accused me privately or publicly in all of these years until after my name was sensationally besmirched by McCarthy.

I now wish to add two other bits of evidence to show that Budenz's testimony is not entitled to credit:

First: Budenz says that he received his list of names as Managing Editor of the *Daily Worker*. I offer for your record an affidavit of James S. Glaser, obtained by my attorneys. I should like to read the text of that affidavit into the record.

UNITED STATES OF AMERICA ⎱
⎰ ss
DISTRICT OF COLUMBIA

JAMES S. GLASER, being first duly sworn, deposes and says:

I am presently engaged in newspaper work in New York City. I am not a Communist Party member and have no relationship with the Communist Party. I was a member of the party until I left it in 1936. From July

1934 to July 1936 I was managing editor of the *Daily Worker*. For many months during that period Louis F. Budenz served under me and received all instructions from me.

During the period July 1934 to July 1936 I was also an ex officio member of the Politburo, top body of the Communist Party in this country.

As the managing editor it was my task to see that the policies of the Communist Party were carried out in the news pages and the editorial section of the paper.

At no time during my tenure was I given names or lists of names by anyone to bear in mind for purposes outside of the regular routine of getting out the paper.

Giving instructions to party members, except for newspaper activity, was the work of other functionaries and at no time a duty of the managing editor.

Finally, as I remember, the staff members of the newspaper, including the managing editor, were never required to keep or retain in memory any list or lists of names.

/ s /   James S. Glaser
_____

Subscribed and sworn to before me this 25th day of April, 1950.

/ s /   Marguerite E. O'Brien
_____
Notary Public, D. C.

This affidavit had been voluntarily submitted by Mr. Glaser for exactly the same motives of good citizenship that had impelled Dr. Dodd to come to the aid of a complete stranger.

Second, it is my understanding that Whittaker Chambers is reputed to have been the key Communist Party link with the State Department. Presumably, if the charges of Budenz and McCarthy have any basis in fact, Chambers would at least have known of me. But I quote from Chambers's sworn testimony before the House Un-American Activities Committee on August 3, 1948, page 575:

QUESTION (by Mr. Stripling, Investigator for the Committee): Do you know an individual named Owen Lattimore?
ANSWER (Mr. Chambers): "No, I don't."

Now, gentlemen, I know that against this overwhelming evidence of this man Budenz's complete unreliability is the fact that he has been used by the Department of Justice as a witness in various cases involving Communists. I call your attention, however, to several considerations in this respect. First, I am informed that the Department has never used Budenz as a witness in any case except against open and known Communist Party members and on the theory, objectives and operations of the Communist Party. Second, I am sure that the Federal Bureau of Investigation has used him, and anybody else it could find as a source of leads, good or bad, for further investigation. Third, I am informed that the Department does not vouch for the general character or credibility of its witnesses. At the most it impliedly represents that it believes that they are qualified to testify on the matters as to which they are questioned. For example, in appropriate cases, it calls as government witnesses, narcotics peddlers, gangsters, racketeers, confessed murderers and thugs.

Gentlemen, I trust that this analysis has thoroughly disposed of the Budenz charges, and also of the scurrilous attacks upon me by Senator McCarthy. But I hope that you will understand that I want to prove, once and for all time, that

I am and have always been an objective scholar and writer, devoted only to pursuit of the truth and subject to no influence or discipline whatever.

It is for this reason that I turn now to the charge that the magazine *Pacific Affairs*, which I edited from 1934 to 1941, was a medium for pro-Communist propaganda.

This charge, gentlemen, is obviously traceable to the same polluted source, Kohlberg's China Lobby, which has attempted to smear me through McCarthy and now through Budenz. The mouthpiece changes, but the tune stays the same. As you yourself have seen, Mr. Chairman, from the document supplied to you by the Institute of Pacific Relations,* these charges are the same as those previously made by Kohlberg against the I.P.R. in a vindictive but unsuccessful attempt to discredit that organization. I would like to emphasize that this analysis was not made by me, now, but was made *five years ago* by officers and trustees of the American I.P.R.

Pacific Affairs, gentlemen, is the quarterly journal published by the international secretariat of the Institute of Pacific Relations. Since it is an international journal, it has always tried to present a variety of authors of different nationality and different points of view.

I make no apology for the fact that under my editorship the magazine carried a few contributions by writers who were then or subsequently regarded as leftist. A writer like Anna Louise Strong, for example, who wrote an article in the June, 1941 issue, was able to present important, first-hand impressions of the Chinese Communist areas when few other outsiders had ever seen them. Her books, and others

* An Analysis of Mr. Alfred Kohlberg's Charges Against the Institute of Pacific Relations. American I.P.R., New York, Sept. 1946. (Mimeographed.)

by writers like her, have been published by reputable publishing houses for years and widely reviewed and discussed. Mrs. Strong has since then been expelled from the Soviet Union; I have always believed that it was one of the strengths of our American system that we do not — in spite of Senator McCarthy — operate that way in the United States.

Pacific Affairs never promoted either Chinese or Russian Communism. It never called Chinese Communists "agrarian reformers." Only one article in the history of the magazine ever used a phrase even resembling this — "agrarian democracy." And an introductory note to this article, which was a translation from the Chinese, made it clear to the reader that the material represented a Chinese Communist point of view.

May I remind you that throughout this period there was nothing reprehensible or even unusual about the occasional publication of significant left-wing views or the analysis of left-wing movements in Far Eastern countries? Such views and analyses appeared in all the leading journals of the United States and the whole western world. In those days, before Kohlberg, McCarthy and Budenz undertook to revise the American tradition of free inquiry and free speech, nobody dreamed of accusing an editor or publisher of being a Russian spy because such views were printed.

And between 1934 and 1941, when I was editor, we published at least 94 contributions out of a total of 250 that were definitely to the right of center. About 147 articles were bibliographies and articles on history, economics, agriculture and other subjects that were neither right nor left. Among our right-wing or anti-Russian contributors were Sir Charles Bell, British authority on Tibet and Mongolia; L. E. Hubbard, a Bank of England economist specializing on Russia; Professor Robert J. Kerner of the University of California; Nicholas

Roosevelt; Elizabeth Boody Schumpeter, who was against a tough policy toward Japan; Arnold J. Toynbee; F. W. Eggleston, later Australian Minister to China; G. E. Hubbard, British authority on China; William Henry Chamberlin, and a strong representation of Kuomintang writers.

This, then, is the record of *Pacific Affairs* while I was its editor. If I had really accepted the humiliating assignment of causing that publication to reflect the views of the Communist Party or of any other group or faction, I was certainly a dismal failure. Clearly, the Party comrades should not have taken it lying down.

But there is another test, and probably a more persuasive one. That is the test of my own writings. These show, beyond doubt, that I followed no line but that of my own intelligence. The detailed proof is too voluminous to recount, but I hope you will bear with me while I recite a few highlights.

In his charges from the Senate floor Senator McCarthy, that profound political scientist, said that the Communist line from 1935 to 1939 was pro-Chiang Kai-shek.

But during that same time, I was critical of the Nationalist Government whenever and wherever I thought they were wrong. In 1935 and 1936 I wrote a number of articles on Mongol affairs that were critical of the Chinese policy under Chiang Kai-shek. In the August 1935 issue of *Tien Hsia*, a Chinese magazine, I wrote that the Chinese ought to have a Mongol policy that would convince the Mongols that "association with China can be made more advantageous for the Mongols themselves than association with either Japan or the Soviet Union." This and other articles caused the Russians to accuse me of favoring Japanese imperialism.

In 1936, in Moscow, I disagreed with the Russian experts on the whole question of Mongolia. In *Pacific Affairs*,

June, 1937, I criticized two Russian articles on politics in Inner Mongolia, one of them by Voitinsky, a top Russian writer on the Far East. Voitinsky called Te Wang, the Inner Mongolian nationalist, a "reactionary." I praised Te Wang, a close friend of mine, for attempting "a democratic coalition of Mongol nationalists."

The Russians thought well of a Kuomintang general named Fu Tso-yi. I criticized him severely. Ten years later this general whom the Russians praised made a deal with the Chinese Communists; while my friend, Te Wang, is listed by the Chinese Communists as a war criminal.

In these years the Communists, of course, hoped that the Japanese assault upon China would strengthen the Chinese Communists. I, on the other hand, kept demanding a tougher American policy toward Japan and kept warning people that unchecked Japanese aggression was building up Communism. In *Amerasia*, December, 1938, I wrote: "Backing Japan today . . . can only mean Bolshevism in Asia."

From 1939, after the Hitler-Stalin pact, according to Senator McCarthy, the Communists turned anti-Chiang until after Hitler invaded Russia in June, 1941.

In 1939 I published very little, because I was finishing a book called *Inner Asian Frontiers of China* — a book that was later translated into Chinese in Chungking, but has never been translated in any Communist country that I ever heard of. In the winter of 1939–40, after Russia's invasion of Finland, I was a member of the local Baltimore committee for aid to Finland.

In 1940, the Communists wanted American policy to parallel that of Russia. I wrote, in *Amerasia*, August, 1940, that we would not get anywhere "by trying to decide whether we should have a policy 'parallel' with Britain or 'parallel' with Russia. What America must decide is whether to back a

Japan that is bound to lose, or a China that is bound to win."

On September 30, 1940, I wrote in a personal letter to Admiral Harry E. Yarnell: "I do not think it is practical politics to negotiate with the Russians about their ideas and our ideas of the future of the Far East. There is too little in common between the two nations on such elementary things as the meaning of words." This, let me point out, was a long time before other people began to refer to the difference in the meaning of words between us and the Russians.

In the spring issue of *Virginia Quarterly Review*, 1940, I urged that American policy should give the government of Chiang Kai-shek the kind of support that "would give the Chinese regular army and the Kuomintang the degree of help they need to maintain their ascendancy under Chiang Kai-shek," and "guarantee that the Chinese Communists remain in a secondary position, because it would strengthen those Chinese who are opposed to Communism."

In June, 1941, just before the German attack on Russia, when Communist hostility to Britain was most violent, I praised the British for their recovery after Dunkirk, and "a morale . . . which enabled the people to face courageously a still dark future."

The next significant date is the year 1943, when Senator McCarthy specifically accuses me of following a switch in the Communist line, attacking Chiang Kai-shek. The truth is once more the exact opposite. In that very year I published *America and Asia*, in which I referred to Chiang Kai-shek and said that "throughout an already long political career he has grown steadily greater and greater."

It was also in 1943 that my wife and I wrote *The Making of Modern China*, published in 1944, in which we summarized Kuomintang history in a way that did not please the Communists. This book was republished in 1947, under the title

China, A Short History. In spite of this opportunity to change our minds and tag along after the Communists, my wife and I included the same comments.

There is one more test on China policy. The Communists attacked General Marshall's mission in China just as Kohlberg and McCarthy are now doing. The Communists accused him of double-dealing. In April, 1946, while General Marshall was still in China, I wrote in a syndicated newspaper article: "His policy can be unreservedly described as in the American interest as well as in the Chinese interest." Over *Town Meeting of the Air*, on the first anniversary of General Marshall's famous report on China, January 6, 1948, I broadcast the opinion that General Marshall's mission was his "first brilliant success as a diplomat." An American Marxist publication, *Science and Society*, criticized my wife and me for "giving General Marshall's famous and ill-fated mission a marshmallow treatment."

The truth is, gentlemen, that the Communist line has zigzagged all over the map, while I have held what I believe to be a steady course of my own, changing emphasis and direction only as the facts and situation altered.

In some of its twists and turns, the Communist line at times coincided with the course I was following, just as for a time it coincided with the program of the American and British governments in the war against Hitler. This does nothing to prove that the American and British governments, or I as an individual, were Communists. It proves only that at times the Communists, for their own reasons, followed the same course that we did.

There is one additional point that I want to stress. I should like to make it clear beyond any doubt that I did believe for a long time — longer than the facts justified, I am afraid — in the ability of Chiang Kai-shek to stop the advance of

Communism by instituting a few, necessary reforms. I clung to my faith in Chiang's ability to free himself and to revitalize the Nationalist Party until 1946, when I began to support General Marshall's policy of salvaging as much as could be salvaged of the Nationalist Party and the Generalissimo's personal position. General Marshall recognized the futility of this hope before I did; and finally, in 1947, I followed General Marshall in accepting the fact that the Kuomintang was beyond salvage.

Perhaps, with my long years of specialized study, I should have been ahead of General Marshall in seeing the shape of things to come. Perhaps I should have foreseen that the corruption and decay of the Nationalist Party were so far advanced by 1946 that it was useless to write and hope for its salvation. I can explain this lack of foresight only because I had not spent any substantial time in China since 1944; and because, not being consulted by the State Department, I had no access to the intelligence on which the Department was basing its policy.

But certainly, my error was in exactly the *opposite* direction from the Communist position. As you know, during this period the Communists were howling for Chiang's blood. I, however, was striving in every way that I could to advocate support for him as long as there was the faintest hope that his failing touch on the political pulse of China would enable him to build a political following.

Let me now quickly comment upon some aspects of my relations with the Generalissimo which are not covered by my published writings.

China was invaded by Japan in 1937. During that war, I supported the Generalissimo's efforts to hold together the coalition with the Chinese Communists in the war against Japan. I also agreed with him when I was his advisor in 1941 and 1942 that the great problem with the Communists was their alien loyalty. I urged him to solve this problem by drawing over to his side a wider coalition than the Communists could assemble.

Here I gave, as an illustration, a quotation from one of my memoranda to the Generalissimo, and the background for it in relations between China, Russia, and Mongolia.

At the very end of this year 1943 — I had resigned as Chiang's adviser at the end of 1942 — I was notified by Mr. K'ung Ling-kai, the nephew of Madame Chiang Kai-shek, that the Generalissimo and Madame would like to make me a present of $5000. I declined this gift, since I was an American government servant who could not properly receive such a gift.

The essential part of this correspondence was the following letter from K'ung Ling-kai:

K'UNG LING-KAI

December 28, 1943

DEAR MR. LATTIMORE:

I have just received a message from Chungking asking me to send to you the sum of $5,000.00 from the Generalissimo and Madame and therefore write to inquire in what form would you wish me to send the funds to you.

With best regards,
Yours sincerely,
(signed) K'UNG LING-KAI

Mr. Owen Lattimore
Office of War Information
San Francisco, California

The wording of this letter could be construed as an offer to remit me the money in some "discreet" way, either in order to disguise the source of the money, or perhaps to enable me to evade income tax. It suggests the possibility that Chinese funds may now be flowing into the China Lobby through concealed channels, and it also suggests that I could, if I had wanted to, have got in on the ground floor of the China Lobby.

Now, gentlemen, I realize that it might be possible to select passages from the writings of a man who is the author of eleven books and more than a hundred magazine articles and hundreds of newspaper articles, to prove almost anything. I think that the best judges of my position, however, are the people who have read my books and articles. I have not the slightest desire to prove innocence by association, which I regard as about as fallacious as trying to prove guilt by association.

In the mass of mail that has come to me since McCarthy's first attack there are over 200 letters from people who have a professional knowledge of my writings and work and of the Far East. Some of these people completely disagree with my analysis and conclusions; some partially disagree with me. But all of them unite in the conclusion that there is nothing in my writings which indicates in any manner that I am subversive or a Communist agent or fellow traveler, or that anything that I have written provides a basis for questioning my integrity or loyalty. It would be insulting even to compare the quality of their judgment with that of McCarthy or Budenz who are brazenly illiterate in the field where they presume to judge.

These people, I suggested, were best qualified to appraise my views and my independence. I quoted from some of their letters and telegrams, and offered the full list to the Committee.

It is, of course, highly distasteful to me to call anyone to witness to my integrity and loyalty. My life and works should be, and I believe are, sufficient evidence of these qualities. But as I read letters from my colleagues all over the country, I realize even more keenly than before that my obligation is to do everything that I can, by the emphatic and conclusive refutation of these charges, to establish, beyond question, beyond dispute, and beyond further challenge, the right of American scholars and authors to think, talk and write, freely and honestly, without the paralyzing fear of the kind of attack to which I have been subjected. [At this point the applause was so loud and sustained that Senator Tydings had to call for order.]

I do not want to exaggerate the importance of my own role or of my own situation here. But as I read the letters that have come to me and as I talk with my colleagues, I cannot fail to note their great apprehension concerning the peril to free research and scholarship which this vicious, political and fanatical attack represents. I want to read to you an excerpt from only one of the many letters that reflect this fear. This is from Dr. Adda B. Bozeman, Professor of International Relations and Comparative Law at Sarah Lawrence College. I quote from a letter that she wrote to Senator Tydings, a copy of which she sent to me:

> Ever since your Committee began its hearings on Senator McCarthy's charges regarding Professor Owen Lattimore I have had difficulties going about the ordinary business of living and teaching.
>
> As a college teacher who began her career ten years ago with considerable enthusiasm, I now spend most

of my energy fighting frustration and futility in the face of the deliberate attack on all values of research and all honest processes of forming one's opinions which is certainly implicit in the treatment up to now accorded to Dr. Lattimore. There seems indeed little use in one's efforts to uphold and develop among students standards of integrity and independence, if a man known for learning and intellectual integrity like Mr. Lattimore can be subjected to the ignominious procedures involved in this case. . . . After several weeks of fruitless reflections about this case and its alarming implications for freedom and security throughout the United States, I have decided to take the liberty of writing to you.

I have not the honour of being included among Dr. Lattimore's personal friends. This letter is, therefore, not really motivated by feelings of personal concern for Dr. Lattimore. I have, however, read most of his books and many of his articles. Although I am not an expert in Far Eastern affairs, I am sufficiently well informed and critically inclined to say that I have at no time and nowhere found a trace of "pro-Communist" or "anti-American" orientation.

Gentlemen, you cannot, you must not permit a psychology of fear to paralyze the scholars and writers of this nation. In a remarkable letter to me, the great Professor Zechariah Chafee of Harvard — an expert on this sort of suppression of freedom — speaks of this McCarthy attack as a "barbarian invasion." It is just that; and the danger of suppressing freedom of scholarship and opinion is, of course, not merely a threat to scholars, it is a direct and immediate danger to the national interest. Attacks of this sort which have the effect of intimidating scholars and researchers are bound to affect the quality of their work, to circumscribe their sources of information and to inhibit the freedom with which they state their facts and conclusions. Particularly is this a calamity with respect to the Far East where our knowledge is pitifully inadequate and our qualified experts woefully few in number.

Senators, I believe that I have dealt with all of the so-called evidence that has been presented in this unprincipled attack upon me. In his press conference on March 22, McCarthy said about my case: "I am willing to stand or fall on this one. If I am shown to be wrong on this I think the subcommittee would be justified in not taking my other cases too seriously. If they find I am one hundred per cent right — as they will — it should convince them of the seriousness of the situation."

Now, gentlemen, I think you have many independent reasons for not taking seriously McCarthy's charges in his other cases. I have little firsthand knowledge of State Department personnel, but I am now something of an expert on McCarthy, Kohlberg, Budenz and their associates.

I know that there are people who have been so misled by the spurious sensationalism of Joe McCarthy that they will not be satisfied unless you produce at least one victim. But I say to you, as a free and independent American citizen, that you have an obligation to yourselves, your high office and your nation which I believe is historic and important. It is, of course, your obligation to clear the individuals who have been unjustly slandered by this man McCarthy. Your task, however, does not cease with the vindication of the individual victims of McCarthy; your task will not terminate even by giving a clean bill of health to the State Department personnel if they deserve it, as I hope and believe they do.

I suggest — and I am sure that intelligent Americans will join with me — that it is your solemn duty to point out, in clear and unambiguous terms, that the processes of the Senate of the United States have been debased by this man McCarthy; that he has been contemptuous of this Committee; that he has lied, distorted and vilified; that he has improperly received and used classified information; that he has made promises which he has not fulfilled; that he has used discreditable and disreputable sources of false information; that he has disgraced his party and the people of his state and nation; and that he has grievously prejudiced the interests of our country.

I suggest that it is your solemn obligation to warn such professional character-assassins that they will not be permitted to run riot or to spread publicly their venom. Those who sponsor these underworld characters who have emerged from a life of violence and conspiracy can do and are doing great damage to our nation. They do not reflect the great American traditions of freedom, decency and faith in one's fellow man. They are unwilling to seek to gain their purposes by the democratic and honorable methods of open debate. To gain their ends — whether those ends are sinister, fanatical or ideological — they use the weapons of personal attack and character-assassination. They are masters of the dark techniques of villainy. They are artists of conspiracy. They are embittered, ruthless and unprincipled.

The net effect of their techniques is to create in this land suspicion and hostility, and to turn citizen against citizen. The result of their work is to circumvent and impede the duly constituted processes of government which should be carefully devised to protect the innocent and to punish only those who are and can be proven guilty. Unless stopped, these persons will destroy the warm faith of each man in his fellow — a credo which is the bedrock of this democracy.

I think that it is important, gentlemen, that this nation,

while continuing its forthright resistance to Communism, should also make sure that it is adequately protecting itself against those few but virulent people in our midst who seek to use the anti-Communist drive as an instrument for their own particular subversion of American ideals.

There is a Chinese saying, gentlemen, that in guarding against the tiger at the front door you should not let your attention be distracted from the wolf at the back door. I urge that we take care of both the wolf and the tiger. This Committee has a unique opportunity to make this great contribution to the national welfare.

I suggest, too, that your Committee and the Congress now reiterate, in the clearest terms, the fundamental American safeguards for freedom of speech and opinion; that you make it plain, beyond dispute, that these fundamental values have not been impaired by McCarthy and his associates; and that you advise all of the scholars, writers and people of this country, that they may and must speak their honest minds with frankness and vigor, and that they will not be vilified for doing so. If this McCarthy nonsense intimidates our scholars and writers, gentlemen, I assure you that the wellspring of democracy will dry up, and that the nation will indeed be in peril.

And finally, gentlemen, I suggest that you put an end to this nonsense of trying to find or manufacture a personal scapegoat for the trials and tribulations of our world position. All of us should concentrate on the crucial problems of international policy that must be resolved if we are to survive as a world power.

Senators, it is plain to all that this country suffered a disaster of the first magnitude when China passed under the control of the Communists. But the question is, what do we do now?

The two great blocs of power to be balanced in the world are those of the United States and Russia. But there is more of the world that is not under the full control of either the United States or Russia, than there is divided between the two of them.

Mr. Walter Lippmann, in the April number of *Atlantic Monthly*, has given it as his opinion that the master key to world policy now lies in our ability to understand and deal with a group of nations that will be independent of control both from Moscow and from Washington. I agree with him.

Mr. Lippmann points out that there is only one idea on which the Communist and the non-Communist world have been in agreement. That is the idea or dogma — I quote Mr. Lippmann's words — "that the world must, and that the world will, align itself in two camps, the one directed from Moscow and the other from Washington."

I agree with Mr. Lippmann that this obsession with a two-way division of the world is Communist dogma, and that too many Americans, while believing themselves anti-Communist, have made the mistake of blindly taking over this Communist dogma.

I myself, however, can honestly say that I have never been the victim of this obsession, in either its Communist or its reflected form. As long ago as 1945, in *Solution in Asia*, I pointed to the coming three-way division of the world. I quote from page 196:

"The world is now grouped in three major divisions. In one, the capitalist economic system and democratic political systems are vigorous and unshaken. In another the Communist (or strictly speaking the socialist) political system is now permanently established, and identified with a collectivist economic system. In the third, there is an adjustment yet to be made between capitalism and collectivism, and mixed political orders have not yet clearly taken shape. There will be a number of them, showing many degrees of modification, and the greatest of all the problems of our time is to work out methods of adjustment and avoid irreconcilable divisions both within countries and between countries."

As the first priority in handling situations of this kind I recommend in my book, *Situation in Asia*, published last year, "virtual alliance with Britain" — hardly, Senators, a Communist idea. I pointed out that the North Atlantic Pact — which the Communists hate worse than they hate the Marshall Plan — would form the nucleus of an alliance. I then added, on page 227, the recommendation that "Only by working through the United Nations can the third countries, which are already critically important in Asia and may become important in Europe, be brought closer to the American side than to the Russian side."

On page 237 I pointed out that policies of this kind "would enable us to take up the adjustment of our relations with Russia backed by the goodwill of countries independent of us but benefiting by association with us, and therefore having a vested interest in remaining free of control by Russia."

Mr. Chairman, just in the last few days there has been published a book, *Peace or War* by Mr. John Foster Dulles (Macmillan, 1950), which, in Mr. Dulles's own way, reflects the same kind of opinion that Mr. Lippmann has been expressing, about the necessity for American policy to adjust itself to associations freely arrived at, with nations which we do not control and to abandon the idea that the only form of power politics is outright control of nations over which we can crack the whip. Now, one thing has certainly been overwhelmingly presented to this Committee, namely, the proof that I am not the architect of the Far Eastern policy of this administration. The latest confirmation of that comes from no less than four Secretaries of State, past and present. But in view of the trend that Mr. Lippmann and Mr. John Foster Dulles are now following, I think, Senators, perhaps I ought to reserve the right to file a claim to be the architect of the Republican Party's foreign policy.

This mention of the four Secretaries of State was a reference to the fact that Senator Tydings had placed in the record a letter he had written to Mr. Cordell Hull, Mr. James F. Byrnes, General George C. Marshall, and Mr. Dean Acheson. In reply to this letter all four distinguished gentlemen had wheeled into line and discharged a volley to the effect that they had never known me and I had never slipped anything over on them. What astonished me most was that not one of them made a simple forthright statement to the effect that he made his own foreign policy, drew on what advice he saw fit in doing so, and took the responsibility for it.

I believe, Senators, that this country is now working toward a policy of this general kind. I believe it will in time be successful. I believe that it can even, in time, be extended to China, relieve China from domination by Russia, and considerably improve our position in Asia. It is true that there have been mistakes in our policy that will have to be remedied. But not only can we, eventually, cut losses. We can make gains — very big and important gains.

But in order to straighten out the disadvantages in our foreign policy and exploit the advantages, one thing is essential. The independent research worker who goes abroad to gather and study facts, as well as the men and women in the State Department who analyze situations and make policy recommendations, must be free to discuss facts, and to present differing opinions, without baseless accusations of disloyalty if their facts or opinions are not pleasing to pressure groups. This is a question that affects the whole fabric of our tradition of freedom of public political debate.

This is also a question, Senators, that vitally affects national security. The collecting of intelligence about other countries ought to be immune from prejudice and emotion. It should be conducted with the coldest realism. The standard of evaluation should not be "will this fact be pleasing to someone who has influence?" but "is this fact true?" Government intelligence agents cannot do a complete job unless they have full and free access to private experts who are in no way dependent, either for pay or for influence, on the federal government. The fact that such experts exist is of incalculable value to the government.

But, Senators, there already exists in Washington and throughout the country an atmosphere of intimidation that is rapidly lowering the quality of research work. Private citizens who are well qualified experts are more and more afraid to express any opinion that may be attacked by a powerful pressure group. Once intimidation has gone as far as this, it is only a short step to the last stage of degeneration. Both private citizens and men in government service begin to be willing to give a little, subtle distortion to their presentation and discussion of facts, in order to please men with prejudices. That is a result of the breaking of the spirit of free men that is fatal to our society.

Gentlemen, I know of no better way to conclude this statement than by quoting from the Congressional Record of July 26, 1949:

> If then we feel it is this important to keep alive in the world the principle of the dignity of man, and our standards of justice and right; if we think it important

enough to sacrifice the lives of hundreds of thousands of young men, and jeopardize the economy of our country by giving away billions of dollars, then it is of utmost importance that we demonstrate at all times to the people of the world that our form of government actually is what we say it is — that it is more fair, more honest, more decent than the governments they have known under Hitler or Stalin, and that our form of government stands for the rights of the individual over and above those of the state.

Surprisingly enough the words that I have quoted were uttered by Joseph McCarthy, the junior Senator from Wisconsin. The Senator, however, gave voice to these eloquent words in the course of a defense of the Nazi SS generals who massacred defenseless American soldiers and a large civilian population in the infamous brutality of Malmédy. For his dubious purpose, the Senator violently denounced the United States Army which he accused of "being guilty of sacrificing the basic principles of American justice." I hope with all my heart that Joe McCarthy will come to understand that the principles of justice and fairness which he loudly proclaimed on behalf of the Nazi murderers are also the birthright of American citizens.

CHAPTER VII

EVEN THOUGH the two statements I had read had been very long it had of course been impossible to discuss many points in detail, and I hoped for an opportunity to say more about my own views and opinions. I was not to get that opportunity.

Senator Hickenlooper, who was really McCarthy's man on the Committee, had already shown that he was interested in trying to build up an impression that I had sinister Communist connections. I was taken aback, however, when I found that Mr. Morgan, the counsel for the Committee, who asked the first questions and whom I had supposed to be an impartial and trained investigator, seemed at times to be motivated by a desire to prove that his zeal in making passes at me with Communist labels, to see if one of them might stick, was not less than that of the Senator from Iowa.

Some of his questions, and some of those I got from members of the Committee, were typical of a state of mind that is dangerous — and infectious. To me the alarming trend in "loyalty" investigations is not the effect of party politics on the conduct of an investigation such as mine, but the fact that competition between the two parties takes the form of each one trying to show that it is more diligent than the other in its willingness to label citizens as Communists. This trend has now gone so far that however convinced individual members of Congress are of the innocence of the individual who has been accused, each one of them feels that his political survival may depend on the fervor with which he displays his own anti-Communism. Under this compulsion, all too often, he throws aside the personal integrity that only a few years ago he would have jealously guarded; he not only proceeds on the assumption that the accused person is guilty until he proves himself innocent, but makes it as difficult as possible for him to prove himself innocent.

Fortunately there are senators and representatives of courage and integrity who stand up against this pressure; but the pressure is there, and it is growing. As it builds up, it creates the wolf-pack psychology that made the old New England witch-hunts into a reign of terror: join the pack, or be turned on and torn apart by the pack.

I have no reason to doubt the good faith or honesty of purpose of the Committee counsel. Some of his questions were undoubtedly asked in order to enable me to reply to statements that had been made against me by Budenz in the executive session from which I had been excluded. Others may well have been asked with the friendly — but futile — intention of forestalling questions by Hickenlooper. But some of them led me to believe that pressure from some of the Committee members and critics induced Mr. Morgan to rough me up a bit in order to protect himself against the accusation of being too "soft."

He began with questions probing me on what I had said about Budenz, to see if I would soften anything I had said. I did not. Then he moved on to one of Hickenlooper's favorite approaches — questions that would make it easy for me to set myself up as more of an expert on Russia than I am. If I had done so, I should of course have put myself in a weak position. This trap was also obvious, and I declined to walk into it.

The next questions were designed to trip me up on the use of the word "democracy" in talking about America and talking about Russia. They led up to a passage on page 139 of my book *Solution in Asia* which has been misquoted so often, in attempts to show that I have called Russia "democratic," that I quote it here in full, with key phrases in italics:

> To all of these peoples [neighbors of Russia in Inner Asia] the Russians and the Soviet Union have a great power of attraction.
>
> *In their eyes* — rather doubtfully in the eyes of the older generation, more and more clearly in the eyes of the younger generation — the Soviet Union stands for strategic security, economic prosperity, technological progress, miraculous medicine, free education, equality of opportunity, and democracy: a powerful combination.
>
> The fact that *the Soviet Union also stands for democracy* is not to be overlooked. It stands for democracy because it stands for all the other things.

The phrase "the Soviet Union stands for democracy" (with the word "also" left out) has been used against me tirelessly by the China Lobby — always with the implication that it is a direct statement of my own belief. The statement that the Soviet Union stands for democracy "in their eyes" — in the eyes of close neighbors of the Russians in Asia who are not in contact with any Western democracy, is left out. In the same chapter there was also the statement that, "America has at present the clearest power of attraction for all Asia."

On page 141 of *Solution in Asia* there follows another passage, in which I tried to give American readers an idea about a typical Uighur in Sinkiang, as a non-Chinese subject of the Chinese under Kuomintang rule:

He lives in a village where all the people are Uighurs; but they are ruled over by the Chinese. An Uighur may become headman of the village, but only by appointment of the Chinese authorities, not by election of the Uighurs of the village. If the Chinese authorities open a village school, it is in order to teach Chinese; if there is any propaganda allowed, it is aimed at persuading the Uighurs to stop considering themselves Uighurs and learn to be Chinese. There is no doctor in the village. There are practically no services in return for the taxes paid.

If this Uighur learns — and he has ways of learning — that among his near kinsmen the Soviet Uzbeks, a poor man's children may attend, free, a school at which they are taught in their own language and taught to take pride in their own history and culture; that they may go on to the university and become doctors, engineers, anything in the world; that they may be elected to powerful positions in which they can give orders even to Russians, because Uzbeks and Russians are equal and it depends on a man's position, not his race, whether he gives orders — then he is going to think that the Uzbeks are free and have democracy. If he is then told that in distant America nobody considers that there is either freedom or democracy in the Soviet Union, he is going to shrug his shoul-

ders. He is not in contact with the American system, and for
him it forms no basis of action.

This second passage is never quoted, but I give it here
because it illustrates one of the most profound problems
of our times — a psychological as well as a political problem.
The description of what a native of Central Asia saw across
the Soviet border was not Soviet propaganda. It was fact —
unpalatable perhaps to Americans, but demonstrably true
at that time. Neighbors of the Russians in Asia saw improve-
ments of this kind in Soviet territory, and were excited by
them — especially the younger people. For these same
people America, if they knew about it at all, was a fairy-tale
land, unreal and far away. They had no way to use the
things that America stands for as a guide to action in the
situations in which they actually lived.

Unless we find a way of handling this problem, America
will become, for the growing generation of a large part of
Asia, more and more an imaginary land — a land of day-
dreams, perhaps, but not a land that sets the standards of
what men do in their ordinary lives. Russia will become
more and more the land of reality. We can only get into
the lives of these peoples, eventually, by the propaganda
of action — through things done by Americans that are
beneficial to other peoples — not by the propaganda of
words over the radio, or even words and pictures in
pamphlets or leaflets.

In all the hundreds of questions that I was asked, not one
attempted to find out if I might have any useful ideas
about such real problems. But any number of questions

were trick questions, based on the suspicion that I might be either a victim or an agent of Russian propaganda.

In an unsuccessful attempt to get away from half-baked clichés about ideologies and back to the world of real politics, I cited to Mr. Morgan a recent experience I had in Afghanistan. While I was there I asked all the foreign diplomats I met whether there was any overt Russian propaganda in Afghanistan. They all replied that at the moment there was not — except one experienced European, who told me that at one point, just over the frontier in Soviet territory, there was a boom development going on. A great city was growing. There was industrial activity. Streetcar lines were being expanded farther and farther. There were lots of movies. People who had formerly led very drab lives, as ragged shepherds or farmers plowing with wooden plows, were getting new kinds of jobs that to them were exciting and attractive. This diplomat left it to me to decide whether I thought that such doings by the Russians, in their own territory, constituted "propaganda" in the neighboring territory of Afghanistan. I do; and that is why I believe so intensely in undertakings like the United Nations Technical Assistance program and the American Point Four program — undertakings that help to change men's lives, to make them happier, and to bring them by action into touch with our world and our way of thinking.

Two lines of questioning taken up by Morgan could only be described, in my opinion, as designed to confuse the issues rather than to elicit facts that would clear up the problems before the Committee.

Budenz had testified that he had been told by others that I was a Communist, or under Communist discipline. I had said that he lied. I give the exact wording of one of Morgan's questions on this point: "Well, Dr. Lattimore, it seems to me — and correct me if I am wrong — that Mr. Budenz's testimony related to what he had been told by others, which you could not know, of course, and I am wondering if his stating what he has indicated was told him is a basis for your concluding that his statement was not the truth."

Abe Fortas indignantly intervened, saying: "Oh, now, Mr. Morgan, after all! Your questioning of this witness, it seems to me, is highly objectionable. The last question implies that you, and I know this is not true, attach a greater dignity to hearsay testimony than to direct statements. This witness, Mr. Lattimore, has testified at length as to just what he characterizes as lies in Mr. Budenz's testimony, and if you want him to repeat that statement, I am sure he can oblige you."

But Morgan went on: "I want him to answer my question, Mr. Fortas."

I then answered: "I should like to add, Mr. Morgan, that Budenz testified to hearsay evidence that I was actually carrying out Communist directives and organizing writers on behalf of the Communists. That is a lie. It is a lie if it was told to Budenz, and it is a lie when he repeats it."

Morgan kept pressing. "We are getting now to the point I wanted cleared up for the record. In other words, when you refer to the fact that Mr. Budenz has not told this Committee the truth, you mean that what he says he was told by others is not the truth; is that correct?"

I replied: " 'He says he was told by others.' Now, that has been denied by others. I don't know whether anybody else told Budenz anything or not. I don't know what weight the Committee may place on the testimony of one ex-Communist, or practicing Communist, versus another ex-Communist. My point is that I have been lied about, and Budenz may have invented that right out of whole cloth, or he may have repeated it. I think he has invented it out of whole cloth."

Later, Morgan asked me — and he admitted that he was following up a line of questioning started by Hickenlooper — "How much of your life, your life during your formative years, was spent under local American conditions; let us say up to the age of twenty-one . . ."

This was really an astounding question to be asked of an American before a Committee of United States Senators, in Washington. I had, of course, been born in Washington and taken to China as a baby less than a year old. I had not returned to America until I was twenty-eight. But consider the implications of the question. It is one of the basic assumptions on which American citizenship and patriotism have been built up that a man born a foreigner can become a citizen as loyal as a native-born American. This assumption applies to a man born, say, in Russia, who first reaches America at the age of twenty-eight. But the implication in Morgan's question was that a native-born American who had spent most of his life in China until he was twenty-eight, might not be a loyal American when he returned to his own country.

Morgan showed that this was his implication by asking: ". . . in your writings concerning the Chinese, particularly up in the Mongolian area to which you have referred, has your thought been essentially what is best for the Chinese people, as distinguished from what might be, perhaps, best for the United States of America, if you can distinguish the two?"

One of the implications of this question is that a man may soon be in danger of being called a disloyal American if he thinks that it would be all right for the Chinese people to have what is best for the Chinese people.

Restraining myself, however, I replied simply that many people who have lived for a long time in some country not their own tend to assume that they have a right to tell the people of that country what is good for them, but that I had always tried to avoid that attitude.

Still another question I quote exactly from the transcript:

Mr. Morgan: It has been suggested in testimony before the Committee that perhaps a defect in your writing, if I may use that word charitably, in the sense of these proceedings, is not so much what you have said but what you didn't say. I am wondering —

Mr. Lattimore: Guilt by omission.

There was laughter at this, but the issue is one that is grimly serious. The idea of "guilt by omission" had first been raised by Freda Utley, in her testimony. It is a mirror-reflection of the standards enforced in Russia, where even an academic research worker is required to put propaganda slogans and tag phrases into everything that he publishes. To suggest that the same degrading standard ought to be enforced in America is a danger signal — a warning that ex-Communists can be anti-Russian and still try to put over, in America, exactly the same totalitarian thought control that is a part of the Communist discipline.

The tag end of the afternoon and almost the whole of the next day were taken up with questions by Hickenlooper, in which he touched several new lows. He had found out, for instance, something that Eleanor and I had long forgotten — that in 1943 Eleanor had spoken on China at the Tom Mooney Labor School in San Francisco. According to Hickenlooper it was a Communist school. He produced an advertisement to prove it, from a paper which he described as a Communist paper, and quoted the California Committee on Un-American Activities — *not in 1943 but in 1947* — as listing the school as subversive. In 1943 the country was at the height of the war effort and both Eleanor and I spoke before innumerable groups that were eager to hear about the war in China — churches, schools, colleges, clubs and civic organizations. Neither of us was a professional discoverer of subversive organizations or activities. As far as Eleanor knew, the Tom Mooney School was sponsored by labor unions, and gave evening classes. She and I were then ardent supporters of Chiang Kai-shek, so if there were Communists in the audience they got an earful of Chiang.

Do you think that had any effect on Senator Hickenlooper? Wait till your turn comes.

My lawyers had urged me to treat the members of the Committee politely, and I had assumed that this applied even to Hickenlooper, but this time I told him that I thought the whole attack on me had set several lows in American political life, and that this attempt to attack me through my wife set a new low.

This question of Hickenlooper's raised an issue that is of very great importance not only in loyalty hearings but in all American discussion of politics and current affairs. Which is the more important, that which an American says, or the audience to which he says it? In my opinion it might help to crack the narrow shell in which most Communists appear to live if Communist audiences would more frequently allow themselves to be addressed by speakers who have not a trace of Communism in their thinking, and who are at the same time authorities on the subjects on which they speak.

Another low-level question from Hickenlooper concerned the fact that in 1947 Eleanor and I had taken our son David with us to Europe on a holiday. He had spent part of the summer with us and part of it with a group of students and teachers from his school, and while they were in Prague (nearly a year before the Communist coup) they had attended some events of an international Youth Festival, living in a school building with students from many countries. He was sixteen years old — just the age to be eager to prove that he could get along on his own in a strange country, in spite of the difficulty of language. The whole experience did him an immense amount of good — and that was true also of thousands of other American youngsters who were over in Europe that summer. But one of Hickenlooper's suspicious questions was — "Did he go to Russia?" He didn't; but Hickenlooper certainly succeeded in extending the range of all possible insinuations of guilt — guilt by association, guilt by nonassociation, guilt by commission, guilt by omission, guilt by matrimony and, finally, guilt by paternity. At this point a reporter passed a note to Abe Fortas: "Is Lattimore's dog a Russian wolf-hound?"

One of Hickenlooper's maneuvers was to ask me about six people, one after the other. After each name, he asked me whether I had considered that person a Communist, at the time. I had not. Then, much later in the hearing, he came back to the subject, lumped all six names together and said, "In view of the volumes of public allegations and discussions about these people indicating their at least very, very strong leftish leanings, and in view of your very brilliant and great ability, Doctor, which I am happy to admit and frankly and honestly admit, it is difficult for me to understand how a man of your perception and experience would fail to sense or appreciate the leftish leanings of those particular people. I would not credit — I would not want to credit — you with being naïve."

It is worth while to study this question carefully. It contains no less than seven booby traps.

1. It implies that I had failed to identify these people as leftists, when in fact I had not been asked whether I identified them as leftists, but as Communists.

2. It implies that any "allegation" of leftism is proof of leftism, and that "volumes of allegations" must be proof of extreme leftism.

3. It implies that I knew all of them equally well, whereas I knew one of them chiefly in New York, another chiefly in Chungking, and the others through casual and infrequent encounters.

4. It implies that a man of "very brilliant and great ability" is a tricky man — and this anti-intellectualism is, of course, an essential part of the campaign for thought-control and against independent thinking.

5. It implies that the questioner is himself "frank and honest" — which is open to doubt.

6. It implies that if I am not "brilliant and able" but tricky, then I must be one of those "brilliant and able" people who are, unfortunately, too naïve and innocent for their own good or the good of the public.

7. It implies — and this is the most dangerous booby trap of all — that "left" is an absolute term. But "left" is a relative term. It means different things to different people. It always raises two questions: left of what, and left of when? A man can be left of Taft and still not a leftist to the majority of Americans. A man can be left of Roosevelt, and still, to most Americans, be neither dangerous nor disloyal. "Left of when?" is a question that cuts even deeper. Should the six people listed by Hickenlooper be described as "leftist" in terms of the ways in which they talked or wrote or acted when I knew them, a good many years ago, or in terms of whatever they may be doing now? Were you yourself stirred by the Russian stand at Stalingrad? Did you subscribe to Russian War Relief or maybe join one of its local committees? Did you ever hope that the tremendous pressure for democratic reforms in China might, perhaps, modify both the Stalinism of the Chinese Communists and the "One Nation, one Party, one Leader" extremists of the Kuomintang and make possible a coalition government that would work? Did you ever feel that peace in China

and international co-operation with Russia might save us from a third world war? If so, in what years did you think, act, or feel in those ways?

A list of who said what, when, published by Drew Pearson, shows how vitally important is this question of timing.

In 1942 General MacArthur said: ". . . The hopes of civilization rest on the worthy shoulders of the courageous Russian army."

In 1943 the *New York Times,* in an editorial, wrote: "We can do business with Stalin! And that business will help our political relations with the Russians. . . . a tenth of the human beings of the world are on the way to higher living standards in Russia."

In 1945, in the *Catholic Quarterly,* the Reverend Geo. H. Dunne wrote: "If Europe moves all the way to Communism, it will not be because of Russian intervention, but because of the obstructionist tactics of die-hard reactionaries."

In 1942 the *Chicago Tribune* wrote: "In Russia's fight to survive as a nation lies the great hope of the world for early peace."

In 1943 Captain Eddie Rickenbacker in *Time* magazine was quoted as saying that "Russia is likely to come out of the war the greatest democracy in the world."

In 1944 Admiral William Standley, ex-Ambassador to Russia, said: "I feel confident that we are on the threshold of a postwar period of collaboration in the fullest sense of the word . . . I am confident Marshal Stalin will agree that, when victory is finally won, it will be our duty to transform this fighting alliance into a concordat dedicated to peacetime construction and to the betterment of the commonweal."

To Drew Pearson's list I can add a comment on the Chinese Communists made by General Patrick J. Hurley in 1945: "The Communists are not in fact Communists, they are striving for democratic principles."

In 1945, when I published *Solution in Asia*, I had explored the possibilities of co-operation with Russia within a framework of world agreement under the United Nations — as did many others. In that book, and in earlier and later books, I have frequently emphasized — as did the Catholic priest quoted by Drew Pearson — the fact that die-hard reactionaries do more than Russia does to spread Communism. But that did not help me when my turn came to be smeared. Unwearying efforts were made to prove that my book was straight Communist propaganda — and the accusations were made in a way that would lead the ordinary newspaper reader to assume that the book was published in 1950, not in 1945.

In great part, however, Hickenlooper's questions during this long day gave the impression of a machine gradually running down. More and more of them appeared to be a random listing of names, on the chance that he might run into one that would put him on a trail. Most of the names were completely strange to me.

Eventually, after further questions by Senator McMahon, Senator Lodge, and Senator Green the hearing, which seemed to me interminable, came to an end. It did not come to a definite end. It just petered out.

A full day of questioning is an experience that leaves you feeling beaten to a pulp — not by hard blows, but by a dull, endless pounding. The nervous strain is not one of acute tension, but one of long-drawn-out watchfulness. A very high proportion of the questions asked me put me on my guard, because they seemed obviously not intended to get a clear picture of the facts, or to establish which facts were relevant and which irrelevant, but to lead me into saying something that might be awkward for me. In handling such questions I found myself focusing intently on each question as it was asked, and at the same time trying, with part of my mind, to determine whether it was an isolated question or part of a pattern.

It is easy for the man who is asking questions to arrange them in a pattern, in the hope that the answer to one question may contradict or appear to contradict the answer to some other question. It is not easy to arrange your answers so that they also form a pattern. It was principally for this reason that I felt, after being ground through the mill, that while I had handled the questions quite well enough as far as they concerned me personally, I had not handled as well as I might have the issues concerning other persons whose names were mentioned.

I found this a delicate problem that bothered my conscience. Someone might be mentioned whom I knew only slightly. From what I knew, I might either feel that that person was almost certainly not a Communist, or I might have a very positive conviction that he or she was not a Communist. But how should I handle my answer? A long answer, strongly worded, might give the impression that I knew the person much better than I actually did. Further questioning might show that I did not in fact know the person very well. If so, there would certainly be further questions. "Why are you so positive in your answers? Are you concealing some part of your acquaintance with this person?" I might, in the end, do more harm than good.

In other cases I had made it clear that the people mentioned were old and trusted friends. That ought to carry with it the assurance that I thought them loyal and patriotic. But, since I had been brought before this Committee to answer charges of disloyalty, and since they might also have to appear before the same Committee, should I also have added an outspoken tribute to their services to their country?

The air was so dense with suspicion, the atmosphere of citizens distrusting other citizens had been so successfully created, that I wondered whether it was any longer safe to talk of friendship in the old, comfortable, neighborly American way. I have friends whom I sometimes do not see for a year or two at a time, and yet when we meet again we are as good friends as ever. We all of us also have friends of friends — people whom we do not know nearly so well, but with whom we get along splendidly. But how, in the cramped surroundings of a loyalty hearing, with fear pressing in on all sides, do you speak warmly and naturally of your friends? Will not McCarthy jump up in the Senate and declare: "See? I told you! That's not just friendship. They are bound together in a sinister way. They belong to the same gang!"

I also felt that I had not succeeded in defining clearly enough many of the issues that arose in the hearings — issues concerning the proper place, in American life, of the citizen in his private friendships, his professional activities, and his participation in political life. For that reason, I want now to sum up some of these issues as they were illustrated by my own experience.

CHAPTER VIII

"IT MIGHT BE YOU"

IT WAS ONLY when the hearings were over that the meaning of everything we had been through really began to sink in. Our lives were in a mess, and it was going to take a long time to get things straightened out. Two months out of Eleanor's life, a month out of mine. Students neglected — including those whom I should, at this time of year, have been helping to get ready for their final examinations. Profitable outside lectures canceled, because I could not get away from Washington long enough. Writing assignments dropped. Summer plans neglected. A college in the South, which had bought twenty-five copies of one of my books, and had paid for them in good faith, asked the publishers to take back the books and refund the money. The college received state aid, and was afraid of getting into trouble for using one of my books.

But that was just our private lives. More important, we soon began to realize, was our standing as citizens. I think we both realized most poignantly what we owed to others when at last we came back from Washington. Friends on the faculty of the Johns Hopkins started to organize a dinner for us. Then suddenly it grew, and there was a reception at which I was to speak. The hall was crowded, and loud-speakers were placed outside. That welcome home gave both Eleanor and me a fortified pride in belonging to the academic community, and it was in speaking to this group that I felt I was best able to thank other colleagues and students in schools, colleges, and universities throughout the country.

The friends who pulled us through were our own kind of people. If you yourself are ever smeared, don't count too much on your important friends, if you have any. The more important a man is, the more he himself may be afraid of a smear. My publisher, when he was urging me to write this book, said casually that it was lucky for me that I knew a lot of important people. "If this had happened to anybody else," he said, "he would have had a much tougher time clearing himself." Abe Fortas had started off with the same assumption that anybody who had had such important mud dumped on him must have important friends. One of the first things he asked Eleanor to do was to draw up a list of influential people. When he looked at it, he said, "Good Lord! Don't you know *anybody* important?"

The fact of the matter is that I know very few "important people" as that term is ordinarily used. I do not owe even my knowledge of China and the Far East to important people. It was not until I became advisor to Chiang Kai-shek, after I had already been over twenty years in China, that I knew many influential Chinese. My knowledge of China and Mongolia and Central Asia was not built up by having pull with the right people, but by traveling in the far interior, by studying Chinese and Mongol until I could read and speak and be completely independent of an interpreter, and by making my way on equal terms among merchants, caravan traders, soldiers, bandits, peasants, shepherds, landlords, grain dealers and others who would be nameless to a "visiting fireman" economist or political scientist or diplomat. Then, on this foundation of real life, I built a superstructure of geographical, historical and sociological study.

In the same way, ever since we settled down to live permanently in America I have not depended on pull or influence in getting the material for my books, articles, and university lectures. Least of all have I depended on government "pipelines." Many economists, political scientists, professors, and journalists quite legitimately cultivate government contacts for the purpose of getting "inside" information, or hints on how to interpret news or policy. To have such contacts is perfectly respectable. "Inside" information is rarely the same thing as "secret" information. It is perfectly understandable that when big news breaks in China, for instance, or somewhere else in Asia, a reporter or a writer of "think pieces" who has never been in Asia promptly consults the friends he has been cultivating in the government in order to get a line on what is going on, but I have never worked this way. Because of my long experience I prefer to use documents in Chinese or the publications that my university gets from many parts of Asia. As for day-to-day developments, there are excellent correspondents in China, Japan, and elsewhere in Asia, so I watch the daily papers. In addition to this, friends of mine — and frequently strangers also — write to me or come to look me up when they come home from China or other countries in Asia. All of this helps me to keep abreast of my profession as an expert on Asia, but it does not build up important friendships for me among influential people.

A few important people did come to my aid, of course. But what it comes down to in the end is that you have to depend on the record of your career and your work as much as on your friends. If you have respected your work, by showing self-respect in your career, other people will respect you for it and stand by you; and if the people who know you and your work believe in you, then other people of the same kind will believe in you.

That was the way we found it. First it was our friends in the neighborhood and my colleagues at the Johns Hopkins who began to speak up. Colleagues in other universities quickly joined. Many of them — the majority in fact — were people I had never met, but people who knew my work and had the professional capacity to judge it. John Fairbank, at Harvard, sent out telegrams to a long list of Far Eastern experts all over the country, suggesting that they write to Senator Tydings, the Chairman of the Committee. Only one man failed to respond immediately. Some of them wrote or telegraphed that they disagreed with my opinions, but that they were convinced that those opinions were honestly arrived at, not disloyal, and should not expose me to what Edward A. Weeks, Editor of the *Atlantic Monthly*, called "assassination by guesswork." One of the most forceful of these letters, written to Senator Tydings, was from Paul Linebarger, Professor of Asiatic Politics at the School for Advanced International Studies at Washington, D.C. I quote one paragraph:

There is a case against Lattimore's views. I have tried to make it as a Federal employee, as a G2 Officer in Stilwell's Headquarters, as a Joint Chiefs-of-Staff Liaison Officer to the OWI, and as a post-war private scholar. But the case is one which can be made honestly against the views. To make it a charge against the man reduces our Republican and Democratic processes to absurdity.

He added that "if Lattimore is a master spy, the *Saturday Evening Post* is a voice of Moscow, General Marshall is a traitor, and Elmer Davis a rascal." Fifteen social scientists at the University of Chicago wired to several senators. A letter, signed by forty-eight people, said:

> We, the undersigned individuals, are each professionally concerned with teaching and scholarly research connected with Asiatic studies in the United States, and Owen Lattimore is known to us as a professional colleague in this field. Among us as individuals there is a diversity of personal opinion concerning American foreign policy, and as individual American specialists we also differ among ourselves in the degree to which we agree with Mr. Lattimore's personal views, but we are each fully convinced of his personal integrity as a scholar and his loyalty as an American citizen, and we deplore and condemn the irresponsible presentation to your Committee of unsubstantiated charges against him.

Some of the letters from students gave me even more comfort for the present and courage for the future than the support of my mature colleagues. I will quote only one of them, from a student in California:

> As I have followed the charges made against you and your answers to them, I have felt that my own right to academic freedom as well as those of every other student

in America, was hanging in the balance; was contingent upon the manner in which you conduct your own defense as well as the outcome of the case . . .

Recently I have gradually slipped into doing and saying what is expedient instead of what I believe to be right. But your actions in giving the lie to McCarthy and Company have heartened me. From now on I am going to express my opinions regardless of the consequences . . . I have resolved to do what is right instead of what is expedient to my own well-being. This means trying to counteract the lies about your case by talking to my friends and neighbors, especially on the campus.

There have been hundreds of letters from other people besides professors, teachers, students and writers. But I am myself a teacher and writer, and therefore what stands out for me in the whole grueling experience is pride in my professional colleagues. The university professor, in times like these, stands in an exposed salient. Frequently, even if no charge has been proved against him, he needs only to be successfully smeared to lose his position under conditions which make it difficult for him to find other academic employment; and it is probably more difficult for the unemployed university professor to find some other way of making a living than it is for most people.

Under such pressures, the temptation to keep his skirts clear of a colleague who is being smeared is very great. But that is only one of his problems. Witch-hunting pressures are pressures for the regimentation and control of thought, and they make original and independent thinking dangerous. It becomes perilously easy for a man, in presenting either his facts or his opinions to those in authority, to give them just that little, servile twist that will make him personally safe. The university professor who saves himself in this way does so at terrible cost and danger, in the long run, to the advancement of knowledge, the health of our democratic society, and the security of our state, as well as to his own integrity.

You must toughen yourself to expect, if your turn comes, that some things will be hard to take. We found that a few people whom we had liked turned out to have been friends to our faces and enemies behind our backs. A few people, whose ability to make a sane, independent judgment we had taken for granted, turned out to be ready to accept ready-made opinions from sensational headlines, hostile editorials, or a slanted rewrite in one of the weekly magazines. People who have been smeared are sometimes shunned or threatened, but Eleanor and I were fortunately spared these indignities. When we went shopping we got the same friendly and pleasant reception as always, and we were told that in the neighborhood movie house, when a newsreel was shown of me landing in New York — even before I had had a chance to defend myself — I was applauded.

Friends may also be frightened of being "implicated," even if they believe you innocent; or they may want to stand up for you personally, but be afraid of compromising their positions. If you have any friends in government service, they are especially likely to be affected. There is no doubt about the way that Washington has been successfully laid under the grip of fear. It turned my bones soft when personal friends in the government, especially in the State Department, did not dare to write or telephone from the office. Sometimes a friend's wife sent a handwritten note from home — not written on the typewriter, of course.

One friend of ours working in a government agency sent over a quotation from a magazine, which was very useful to me. It was not "classified," of course, and she had no way of knowing that another friend had already sent in the same clipping. That particular magazine is available in libraries and can be bought in bookstores. As a matter of fact, I have it in my own library. But later this friend got to thinking that, as a government employee, she had exposed herself to real danger by helping us at all. She had not violated security. She had done nothing that infringed any kind of regulation. But the terrible thing is that she was quite right — she was in real danger. The state of panic in government agencies is such that she could have been attacked by anybody snooping for McCarthy. If she had been attacked, her intimidated superiors might very well have reprimanded her, instead of defending her.

In my own ordeal by slander it did not take us long to realize that one of the strong points in my favor was that I held no government position and had no ambition to hold one. For this reason McCarthy's attempt to prove that I was masterminding the State Department by remote control fell flat. But, ironically, this was not my only advantage. I also benefited by not having to rely on the weak backing of frightened government officials, or the cautious tactics of government lawyers. I could fight my own fight, with the uncompromising support of my able and fearless lawyers.

There is always the additional danger that people with old personal grudges will give aid and comfort to a witch-hunt. They may be people you have forgotten about for years. Somebody may have imagined that you once slighted him when you never did, or never intended to. And, in all professions, there is always professional jealousy. You are defenseless against the man who is trying to work off a grudge, because everything depends on how mean-spirited he is and how far he is willing to go. I was, I think, extraordinarily lucky. So little personal spite turned up in the way of contributions to McCarthy's poisonous spider-web that it gave me the comforting feeling of having a good record in dealing with my fellow men; but what little spite did turn up was very spiteful, and I recognize that this is a real danger that every man faces.

The fight had hardly begun, however, when I realized that the newspaper picture of McCarthy is misleading. It does not begin to reveal how dangerous he really is. He is usually described as a reckless political gambler and a wild-swinging bruiser who charges into a brawl without sizing up the situation. The truth is that every move he makes is coldly calculated, and that he is the master of a formidable technique. In his impassioned defense of the Nazi SS murderers who massacred unarmed American prisoners and Belgian civilians at Malmédy he drew on pro-Nazi sources of information, and in his use of China Lobby material against me he was again in touch with pro-Nazi propagandists. It is not surprising therefore that so much of the fascist pattern appears in his technique of vilification.

He uses, for instance, the repetitive lie, renewing a charge after it has been disproved, and the alternative lie, switching from one unsupported charge to another. He is also a master of timing, which may be partly due to the fact that he has had skilled journalistic help — notably that of Willard Edwards of the *Chicago Tribune*. By attacking me while I was out of the country he gained the maximum time to exploit his charges. Finally his four-hour speech against me on the Senate floor was so voluminous that it was impossible to deal in full detail with the whole mass of innuendo and misrepresentation in the short time available to me for preparation of my rebuttal. In the amazing bulk of this diatribe we counted ninety-six lies — not wrong opinions but actual misstatements of fact.

The tracking down and full documentation of even one lie can be very time-consuming. One example was the charge that I had belonged to the Maryland Committee for Democratic Rights, described by McCarthy as a subversive organization. Eleanor tracked down the story, and here it is:

Years ago, before Pearl Harbor, an eminently respectable Episcopal clergyman asked me, along with a number of other solid citizens, to sponsor a meeting that was to be held in Baltimore under the auspices of the Maryland Committee for Democratic Rights, at which a Swarthmore professor was to speak. Naturally I accepted; but I did not attend the meeting (much less join the organization), and forgot all about it. Eleanor's research showed that this Maryland group had been affiliated with a national organization called the National Emergency Conference for Democratic Rights, but the Maryland group apparently held only one more meeting, and then expired of sheer lack of animation. Three years after that — *after the Maryland group no longer existed* — the national organization was declared "subversive" by the Attorney General. And *ten years* after I had sponsored that long-forgotten meeting, that sinister fact was brought out to fill in the crudely drawn picture of me as a dangerous and disloyal character!

McCarthy used this trick of guilt by association over and over. Another example was his attempt to associate me with the Writers Congress. In 1943, as the Director of the San Francisco office of O.W.I., I had to speak at all kinds of patriotic and fund-raising rallies. They were quite a heavy tax on my time, involving overtime work when I got back to my office. One such meeting that I attended was a Writers Congress in Los Angeles. I had never heard of it but I went, in the line of government duty. Years later, it was listed by the Attorney General as a subversive organization, and McCarthy, of course, insinuated that my connection with it was subversive. We found that it cost not only a great deal of time but a lot of money to straighten out the long-forgotten details. And when, finally, we had straightened out the record, the fact was not quoted anywhere to show that I had proved a charge against me to be false. It just wasn't important enough to be news. Nor did it have the slightest effect on the smears. Like hounds baying down a false trail, McCarthy and his pack merely yelped "we nearly turned up a real rabbit there!" and kept right on baying down other false trails.

It is a commonplace saying that the man who is accused is at a disadvantage with his accuser when it comes to headlines and newspaper space. This commonplace observation becomes very poignant when you are the man accused, and a man like McCarthy ruthlessly exploits his advantage by making the accusations so sensational that the revelation of the truth seems drab and dull by comparison. All the more, therefore, I realize the debt that the victim of a smear owes to newspapers and individual reporters, commentators, and cartoonists who are not afraid to cut through the allegations and go after the facts.

A few newspaper and radio correspondents knew me personally and were familiar with my writings. The reporting and editorial work of those men were clearly based upon the ancient principle that I was innocent unless proved guilty. Among them were Herbert Elliston, Elmer Davis, Eric Sevareid, Ed Harris, Martin Agronsky, I. F. Stone, and Hamilton Owens. Drew Pearson led off, the moment the news broke, with his reverberating "I happen to know Owen Lattimore personally, and I only wish this country had more patriots like him."

I also owe a very special debt to men I have never met, or had never met before, like Al Friendly of the *Washington Post*, and many other reporters who worked hard and conscientiously to present the facts. I was kept so busy that I never had time to catch up with all the clippings and so I do not yet know all of those whom I should like to thank individually, but as an example of the way they handled my case I must mention at least Edward R. Murrow. Even when the hysteria was at its height, before I could speak for myself, he kept the record straight by repeatedly drawing attention to the fact that nothing had been proved against me. Later, by his program technique of using recordings, he gave me a national forum of my own, so that millions of people could hear me speaking for myself, in excerpts from my testimony.

I was very much encouraged by the editorial support that I found coming from all over the country. The weak spot in the press, however, for those who are in danger of being smeared, is the fact that so many papers show a split personality. Sometimes this is because of party politics, or the religious vote, or sheer timidity, or just because of the kind of conservatism that believes that when it comes to loyalty cases one bed that has had a Red found under it justifies burglarious entry into ten peaceful homes in search of non-existent Reds.

In my own case my home-town paper, the *Baltimore Sun*, gave a good demonstration of split personality. As I have already described, its chief editor, Hamilton Owens, an old friend, came all the way to London to meet me and published an account of my homeward trip that was a comforting boost when the going was tough. Philip Potter, of its Washington staff, did a first-class job of reporting, and Yardley, its cartoonist, did a marvelous portrayal of McCarthy, sweating, getting a dressing-down from "the professor." Finally, when the tough going was over and I was welcomed home by my Johns Hopkins colleagues, it printed a friendly editorial which did not concede that my innocence had been definitely established but did concede that my colleagues liked and respected me. In between, however, one of its editorial writers, C. P. Ives, who also writes a signed column on Monday mornings, printed some amazing contributions on the significance of McCarthyism as he sees it. In one of these, on April 10, he wrote: ". . . the sophisticated people, the delicately educated people, what might be called the prevailing American intelligentsia, have, by and large, left it to the political primitives to alert the American republic against the deadliest threat of its history. . . . By and large, it is the primitives who have spoken an instinctive suspicion which wells out of the inmost hearts of very great numbers of plain and unsophisticated people."

The very wording of this kind of journalism recalls the old Nazi appeal to primitivism — the exhortation to "think with the blood," the encouragement to the mob to intimidate those who think with their brains.

Writing of this kind, despairing of intelligence, education, and informed knowledge, and conceding a mystic, brute wisdom to prejudice and emotion, preceded the rise of Hitler. Nothing more effectively prepares the way for a demand for Authority and a Leader. I do not wonder that I hear so often, from refugees who came here from Europe, the sad and frightened words "this is where we came in."

In taking advantage of Senatorial immunity to get a big spread in the headlines an unscrupulous politician can inflict sudden financial disaster on his victim. While a McCarthy jauntily evades any responsibility for producing solid evidence, the man who is forced to drop his work and appear in Washington to try to clear off the mud with which he has been wantonly splattered may have to meet expenses that easily wipe out the savings and mortgage the future of a university professor or a professional man.

A man cannot defend himself against such an attack easily or alone. Perhaps the greatest costs are to his work, his career, or his health, but the actual financial expenses, to himself and to the friends who come to his assistance, are enormous. In my case they involved cables to Kabul and Karachi, long telephone conversations to London and Shannon, to Nevada and California and Minnesota and

New York, and of course endlessly between Washington and Baltimore. They involved the travel of lawyers and witnesses and friends, and the moving of a household to Washington.

A man who must defend himself is fortunate if he happens to live in Washington so that he can be at home and keep an eye on his job while at the same time he does the hundred things necessary to his defense which can only be done in Washington. He must have a Washington lawyer, with whom he is constantly in touch, because sudden and unexpected moves by his attackers have to be met promptly. For me, even Baltimore was too far away, and while we were exceptionally lucky to be loaned a house in Washington, just the extra expenses, for six weeks, of restaurant meals, taxis and train fares back and forth for me and my volunteer helpers mounted high, on top of keeping our household going in Ruxton. In the end these were small, however, in comparison with the biggest bills. Transcripts of the proceedings needed to prepare my rebuttals, for instance, cost more than three hundred dollars, and the mimeographing of statements, fact sheets and press releases, a total of about two hundred fifty pages, cost over eleven hundred dollars, because much of it had to be done at overtime rates. If it had not been that my wife and I and several volunteer helpers could type, stenographic expenses would have been colossal. Quite apart from lawyers' fees, which for most people would be the largest item of all, and apart from time lost, which can mean heavy financial loss, expenses can quickly run into many thousands of dollars.

I have been fortunate in having unbelievably generous

and public-spirited lawyers who have refused to charge more than their actual expenses, and friends who have offered to contribute to what they consider to be my defense of a common cause. However, while it isn't easy for a man of my age to see his savings disappear it is even more distressing to find himself in a position where he has to accept financial help. Already it has cost some of our friends as well as ourselves more than we can afford, in money as well as time.

And then remember that you get no compensation and no reimbursement whatever for having been unjustly accused. McCarthy, while he was campaigning against me, was employing more people than the investigating committee itself. At one time he claimed to have had help from a staff of thirteen. Later he cockily told the press that he was employing four ex-F.B.I. men and using another part time. In addition he had secretarial and "research" help. He said that he was "doing all right" and getting the money he needed. In contrast to the ability of such a man to inflict costs on an innocent victim, I think that one of the most monstrous and cold-blooded things that Louis F. Budenz said in his testimony was that it was a "Communist" tactic to sue for libel. Not, he added, in order to win, but to "bleed white" the libeler. Who is "bled white" I should like to know, the libeler or the libeled? Remember that Budenz, as well as McCarthy, spoke under Senatorial immunity, because he was appearing as a witness in a Senate hearing. Both men refused to repeat, without the shelter of immunity, the charges they had made under immunity.

It was time-consuming and expensive to dig up all the facts and produce the witnesses to straighten out the record.

But what was really humiliating was the heavy and relentless pressure to produce evidence, not that I had worked from ascertained facts, and not that I had showed professional competence and independent judgment in drawing my conclusions from those facts, but purely and simply that my facts and my conclusions had been of a kind to draw unfavorable adjectives from American and Russian Communists. Senator McMahon was especially insistent that I file with the Committee a full list of denunciations of me by the Russians. His intention was obviously friendly, but it was equally obvious that he did not realize that the whole idea of proving that you are not despicable by listing the people who despise you is deeply humiliating.

As a matter of fact I do happen to have been attacked in the Russian press, sometimes in very strong terms. Eleanor remembered this while I was still in Afghanistan, and managed to find half a dozen book reviews in which I was called "a learned lackey of imperialism," a "libeler of the Chinese Communist Party," and a "servant of Japanese imperialism." One Russian reviewer even said that my "scholasticism is similar to Hamlet's madness." She knew that a further search would turn up more quotations of this kind; though they are hard to find in this country. But these Communist certifications of my anti-Communism were available only because I had written on subjects that happened to interest the Russians. I might easily not have been able to produce a single one — and still be a loyal American.

I was in fact actually handicapped by the fact that I have always written as a social scientist and not as a propagandist or polemicist. I had always taken it for granted that of course, and without question, American policy, in pursuit of the American interest, must aim at limiting the spread of Communism and at encouraging in other parts of the world political institutions and economic structures that would have a vitality of their own to survive against Communism. Everything I ever wrote was based on this assumption. It had not seemed necessary to spell it out, as the Russians have to spell out their creed so constantly and so publicly, with a self-debasing servility. It had never occurred to me that, in order to prove myself a man who was not and had never been a Communist, I ought to adopt the vocabulary of a Communist. But time and again in Washington I found myself running into doubt and hesitancy. "What, no vulgar propaganda? No blood-heating polemics? Sir, do you call yourself a scholar?"

My experience shocked me into realizing the urgency of a problem of which I had already been aware in a general way — the problem of the education and training of experts to handle our business and diplomatic contacts with various parts of the world, in face of the fact that Marxist thinking is widespread and organized Communist Parties have become permanent factors in the political life of many countries. Our experts will have to deal with countries that are under outright Communist control, and others in which the governments, without being Communist, have some Communist theories or some Russian methods.

Looking back, I recall that my own thinking was not formed by any kind of theoretical dogma. The combination of an American family background, education in England, and the maturing effect of early business experience and independent travel among the fascinatingly diverse peoples and conditions of the interior of Asia had given me a taste for observing and comparing facts. I had no intellectual craving for theories out of books. I got enjoyment and satisfaction out of observing facts for myself, selecting those that I thought significant, and exercising my independent judgment in forming my opinions. I thought of all theories as part of the raw material to be examined by the scholar.

My contact with Marxist thinking was secondary and late. I was in my thirties when my studies made it more and more necessary to deal with the Russian frontier in Asia. I was thirty-six when I decided that I had to learn Russian in order to get access to more source material. Thereafter I learned to deal with the Marxist slant in Russian authors just as I had learned to deal with the peculiar theories of all kinds of authors who wrote in English, French, German, Chinese, and Mongol.

But I belonged to the last generation of Americans who could expect to train themselves by such easy, casual methods of gradual growth. The regions in which I traveled so freely when I was younger will be for a long time difficult for Americans to enter. Our future experts on these regions will have to work more in books and less in the field. And they will have to be well trained if they are to be the masters of the books they read instead of being dominated by the authors of the books. Today, a young American who wants to become an expert in the regional studies on which I have worked so long should certainly learn Russian much younger than I did. And he should have a systematic training in the analysis of Marxism, because he cannot compare his Russian books with the facts on the spot as freely as I did, and must therefore know what Russian — or Chinese — Marxist authors are driving at, in order to be able to separate facts from theories and form his own judgment.

How is this to be done while McCarthyism terrorizes our teachers? It is more difficult to think sanely about Marxism and Communism in the United States than in any country in which I have had any experience, but we must face the fact that Marxism is not just a temporary problem, to be dealt with on an emergency basis, but a problem that is going to be a more or less permanent part of our relations with the rest of the world. Marxism is not a new problem that has suddenly burst upon Europe, as it has on America. To hundreds of millions of people in Asia, Communism is not as terrifying as it is to Americans. They have never had any democracy, and have no democracy to lose. Therefore, in comparison with what they have had, Communism doesn't seem so frightening as it does to us. Communism frightens us because our history as a nation has been lived under democracy. We know the benefits of democracy, and we do not want to gamble them against any strange doctrine from abroad.

In comparison with Europe and Asia, Marxism has had little effect on political thinking in Britain, and still less here in America. Why this should be so is a problem that lies outside my field of specialization; but to the limited extent that I check on the writings of American Marxists in the course of my own work, what strikes me as characteristic of them is their mechanical use of slogans and ready-made social, political, and economic formulas borrowed from Europe and Russia. This characteristic, I believe, limits their influence on American thinking. Whether a writer is a Marxist or a disciple of any other "ism," he will not get very far if he merely parrots a theory in order to fill a blank in his own ability to think. Marxism will only become a major influence in American thought if there is a notable increase in the number of Marxists who are able to do their own thinking. That would mean that Marxism had begun to acclimatize itself and to take root in the American environment, as it has not done up to the present — and then it would become a really important factor in American politics.

To forestall this danger, repression is of no use. Outlawing the Communist Party would only make it go underground, where it might flourish more than it does above ground. We must put our reliance where we have always put it — in the vigor and health of our free institutions and in the benefit that those institutions confer on every member of society. America, of all countries in the world, is the one country where democracy has always been, not a word, not a theory, not a pious aspiration, but a living, breathing thing. Our democracy was not created by indoctrination but by practice, and in the long run it will not be preserved by indoctrination but by practice. Each generation of Americans since the Founders has been able to say "Our forefathers had democracy — and we have even more." If we can hand on to our children a democracy that is still vital and growing, there is nothing to fear.

CHAPTER IX

A TIDE OF FEAR has swept Washington and is undermining the freedom of the nation. We cannot turn that tide just by vindicating each individual who has been falsely accused; we must re-establish the freedom to inquire and the freedom to express opinions based on independent inquiry. These two freedoms are the flesh and the spirit of our political and intellectual freedom. Unless they are recognized by more than lip service; unless we can actually enjoy them in practice, the rights of the citizen are doomed.

We have gone through shattering disillusionments since the end of the war and in them is the root of the evils that now haunt us. The fight to save the world from being enslaved by fascism and militarism was won by a Grand Alliance of very different peoples and states and we thought of all our allies as being on the democratic side. We all called each other democratic. The United Nations was founded on the hope that there could be a peacetime association between peoples who had many conflicting interests, but certain fundamental interests in common. We hoped to win the peace by finding ways to reconcile the still remaining conflicts of interest among the peoples of a liberated world.

The disintegration of this wartime Grand Alliance now

threatens to destroy the United Nations and the peace of the world. A great hope has been deferred, and our hearts have been made sick. Fear and suspicion now run wild in our country.

The witch-hunting of which McCarthy is a part is recruited from ex-Communists and pro-Fascists, American Firsters, anti-Semites, Coughlinites, and similar fringe fanatics of the political underworld. It was groups like these that Hitler used to run interference for him, causing the confusion and dismay that he and his real backers, the big-time reactionaries, needed in order to take over the state. But these vanguards of fascism cannot be dismissed as lunatics. Their purposes are diverse, but all of them lead up to the training and indoctrination of strongarm groups. In the meantime they flourish on dissension, turmoil, and notoriety. To keep themselves in the news and to promote the sale of their books and their appearances on radio, television, and lecture platforms they need a never-ending supply of victims. To provide themselves with the victims they need, they resort to a merciless use of "guilt by association." The "experts," especially the ex-Communists and those with fascist leanings, turn out to beat the bushes in a man-hunt for people whom they can conveniently use. Their most important function is not to turn up real Communists, most of whom are already known to the F.B.I., but to assert brazenly that they have a sinister, underworld, instinctive knowledge that the kind of person you are is the kind of person a Communist is.

McCarthyism has not yet been successful in establishing thought control, but it is using well-tried propaganda methods in its effort to do so. In order to stop a well-qualified independent expert from expressing his personal opinion, the McCarthy method is to accuse him of other things. Accuse him of being an espionage agent. Bring in a witness to accuse him, not on the grounds of what the expert has written, but on the ominous suggestion that he "organized" other writers. Accuse him of being the "architect of Far Eastern policy." Throw a bomb which emits clouds of nauseous smoke and then turn in a false fire alarm. The next step is to use the simple propaganda device of insisting over and over again, even weeks after complete evidence has disclosed the false alarm, that where there is so much smoke there must be some fire.

The use of seemingly logical phrases like "no smoke without fire" is only one kind of the dishonest logic which is the most terrifying and deadly technique of the smear charge. Another standard device uses the following pattern: The typical Communist is a man whose thinking is regimented with the thinking of other Communists, but has nothing whatever to do with the thinking of average Americans. Any man who thinks independently is in a minority; since the Communists are also a minority, accuse the independent thinker of being a Communist; then deny that he is thinking independently, and accuse him of being regimented along with the other Communists.

The McCarthy kind of politician resorts to Congressional immunity to build up his charges in a way that would be libelous if first made in the press or on the radio. But once the charge has been made under immunity, the quoting of it does not expose the press and radio to libel actions. A charge made under Congressional immunity has sensational news value. Under a pattern of journalism that has, unfortunately, become frozen and conventional, press and radio are bound to follow up every angle of a sensational charge. But disproof is rarely sensational. An accusation is positive. It asserts that something sinister and exciting exists. Disproof is negative. It merely demonstrates that nothing sinister or exciting exists. If it doesn't exist, it is less "newsworthy" and gets a smaller headline and a smaller story. Since millions of people read only headlines, the accusation persists in the public mind.

The McCarthy demagogues who are working to destroy our traditional liberties have already made great gaps in the tradition of freedom which has made this country unique. They have been working to strengthen and to exploit politically a dark tide of unreasoning, hysterical fear. McCarthyism insists constantly, emotionally, and menacingly that the man who thinks independently thinks dangerously and for an evil, disloyal purpose.

The resulting danger to American democracy is clear and present. We are beginning to reflect in our own conduct that which we abhor in thought control as the Russians enforce it. We are repelled by the servile way in which every Soviet contribution either to the social sciences or to the natural sciences has to be certified by the writing in of paeans on the superiority of Marxism, tributes to Stalin as the source of all wisdom, invective against "bourgeois science," and attacks on scientists in democratic countries as camp followers of "capitalist imperialism."

It is time for us to wake up to the fact that the McCarthy tactics of bullying any man who stands up for an independent opinion are crowding us into setting up a similar vicious standard here in America. More and more we are allowing thought-control questions to be asked. "How long is it since you last denounced the Russians? In your recent monograph on the pottery of the Hopi Indians why did you not insert an irrelevant but zealous glorification of the American Way? Can you produce evidence of having been denounced, within the last six months, by the American Communists? When were you last attacked in a Russian publication?"

The special pressure groups which promote McCarthyism have already succeeded in intimidating Washington to such an extent that fair-minded senators feel they have to be very cautious in coming even indirectly to the aid of its victims by establishing the real facts which disprove the accusations. They are political men, and they feel that they are in real danger if they attempt to go against a political tide. The pressure on them is made heavier by the fact that the Republicans are trying to stake out a claim to be the Kremlin of anti-Russian and anti-Communist ideology. The Democrats, in reply, are trying to show that they are just as anti-Russian and anti-Communist as the Republicans. As a result, both parties are to an alarming extent neglecting the most vital issue, which is the maintenance of democratic standards and practices in the face of *both* Communism and the demagoguery of the witch-hunters.

Most newspapers, moreover, are Republican or Democrat, and like congressmen and senators they feel the pressure either to prove that the Republicans are the noblest Red-catchers of them all or that the Democrats are not a step behind them on the trail of blood. Because some newspapers, radio programs, and motion pictures have helped to swell the tide of emotion and panic, all of them are now in danger of being swept away by it.

Bully-boy politicians of the McCarthy stripe were the forerunners who softened up Germany for the coming of Hitler. They are demagogues who are skilled in the exploitation of fear. They aim at more than the intimidation of the individual. If the individual can be successfully intimidated, then whole areas of timidity can be created among politicians, in the press, on the radio, in the moving picture industry, and in schools and colleges. We have the grave and recent warning of history that once a whole society has been softened up in this way it is easy to create a demand for a leader who will resolve the confusion, impose conformity and regimentation, and install the fascism that is the final ambition of the demagogues.

The standards that the witch-hunters are trying to impose on us are the standards of propaganda, of mob thinking, and of thought control. They have no place in a free atmosphere of individual and independent thinking. We are therefore deeply involved in a double emergency. Within our own country, our traditional freedoms are being paralyzed by fear fostered by organized pressure groups which are hard at work to deepen the intimidation and make the paralysis more rigid. Beyond the shores of our own country, all the many constructive possibilities of our foreign policy are being frozen by the cold war. The freeze is already so deep that nothing is left of foreign policy but the cold war itself. And yet it should be obvious that the cold war offers no solution either for our own problems or for the problems of the world.

To find an escape from this emergency we must do two things. Within our own country, we must break the paralysis of fear and win our way back to the traditional American freedom to think and on the basis of independent thinking to express independent opinions. Beyond our shores, we must use this reasserted freedom in a grand attack on the problems of the cold war. We cannot say that one of these things ought to be done first and the other second. We must do both at the same time. We cannot first win freedom from fear at home and then exercise that freedom in an attempt to find a new and better foreign policy, nor can we try to end the cold war and then, with fear and suspicion lightened through the world, try to win freedom from fear at home. We can only succeed if we free ourselves from fear and win back our freedom to think, and in the very act of so doing make use of our freedom to think by boldly setting ourselves to the task of thinking our way out of the cold war.

We must, to begin with, do some fresh thinking about the problem of Communism, both in foreign policy and at home in America. We have already so deeply conditioned ourselves, psychologically, to using the word "Communism" as a danger signal to distinguish between countries that we can deal with and countries that we cannot deal with that we are going to find it hard to carry on a reasonable debate about our problems. We should take as an example and a warning the difficulty and delay we encountered in working out a sensible and practical policy toward Yugoslavia. Because the word "Communist" has a hypnotic effect on newspapers the State Department is always in danger of criticism if it uses common sense in taking advantage of the fact that there are Communists in Yugoslavia and a number of other countries who are at the same time independent nationalists, and will therefore find ways of getting along with us if we show more respect for their independence than Russia does. The latest and greatest disaster in our foreign policy is another example of the hypnotic use of the word "Communist." By the violence of their objection to a government with even a few Communists in it the China Lobby and its friends in the Congress prevented us from helping to bring into being a moderate government in China and forced us to follow a policy that resulted in putting China completely under the power of the Communists. Demanding that we follow that policy to the bitter end, they are now in fact making us force China into complete alliance with and dependence on Russia.

In the future we are not going to be able to deal any better or any more promptly with such problems as these unless the people in America who study and write about them can safely engage in public debate without the threat of persecution for those who hold minority opinions. Our experts must be allowed to translate, publish, and discuss the writings of Russian, Chinese, and other Communists. They must be allowed to recognize that, regardless of whether the theories of these Communists are right or wrong, they are the theories that shape the lives of hundreds of millions of people under Communist rule. To that extent they are not only theories but political actualities, and must be dealt with as such. It will be the death knell of our democracy if we allow the McCarthys and such pressure groups as the China Lobby to establish a party line of knowledge in such matters. Research must not be bounded by any kind of political doctrine. When the presentation of unpalatable knowledge becomes dangerous to the individual, the state itself is endangered.

The problems raised for us by Communism in Russia, Communism in countries not controlled by Russia, and the fact that there are also Communists in America are going to interact on each other in the future as do many other internal and external problems. This complex of problems will require American research workers, social scientists, and publicists to set strict standards for themselves, to defend these standards, and to establish a place for them in American public opinion.

Marxism and sub-varieties of Marxism are going to play a continuing part and a more and more complicated part in the world's affairs. Our national security in dealing with other countries, and also the health and vigor of our own political life at home, require careful study of Marxism in all its forms and all its divergent political organizations.

We cannot, for our own safety, entrust the expert study of Marxism only to reactionaries who are opposed to all forms of liberalism as well as to Marxism. Still less can we afford to place ourselves in the hands of people whose claim to be experts rests solely on the fact that they are ex-Communists. It is extremely rare to find an ex-Communist who is dispassionate enough to be able to keep separate his change of ideas and his personal antagonism toward people whose ideas he used to share. We certainly cannot afford to entrust the assessment of ideas, either in foreign policy or in politics at home, to men of whom we are never sure whether they are honestly treating ideas as ideas, or pursuing personal vengeance against individuals or cliques among their former associates.

It is a perversion of all common sense to make renegades into heroes of our society, but McCarthyism has progressed so far that Senator Chavez has referred to the bitter fact that the man who has never been a Communist is being reduced to a low status because he cannot, like the ex-Communist, produce a certificate of former membership in the Communist Party. Moreover, we should remember that a Communist who has left the Communist Party may have genuinely quarreled with his former comrades and yet still be a subversive revolutionary, differing from other Communists merely in sectarian dogma.

The renegade Communist, like a deserter from the enemy in war, has a limited value for intelligence purposes which is greatest when he has just deserted. During the current tide of fear, however, a man who was high up in the Communist Party ten years ago is often consulted as if he were an authority on the inner workings of the Communist high command today — which he is not and cannot be.

It is not ex-Communists but independent researchers with a tradition of free expression who have made the most authoritative analyses and predictions of Marxism and Communist policy. In the long run a democracy must rely on independent, non-renegade experts as the only experts who can make a conscious and sustained effort to see things in perspective.

We are in one of those national crises in which the fundamental cause of liberty will either be seriously impaired or renewed and strengthened, depending on what we do. To break the grip of fear we must revive both the letter and the spirit of the Bill of Rights, which have been violated by the witch-hunting method of intimidating government personnel and private citizens by denunciation. The United States was founded in a period of crisis, and men experienced in crisis hysteria insisted on adding to the Constitution provisions intended to protect citizens from unjustifiable prosecution.

The Bill of Rights that they wrote was sharply devised to meet the dangers of unjust arrest and imprisonment without trial — the principal dangers to which citizens were exposed in those days whenever there was a wave of mass hysteria or official persecution. A modern addition to that kind of danger is persecution by denunciation. Because of the media of mass publicity, such as the press and radio — particularly when a member of the Congress provides the occasion by abuse of the privilege of immunity, this kind of persecution and intimidation now goes on unchecked. Unless we see to it that persecution by denunciation is not allowed to happen here, we shall soon find that the Bill of Rights is a monument to the past rather than a bulwark against present evils.

The standards of Congressional investigation should be brought into line with modern requirements. A Senatorial committee of investigation works in a manner which is not comparable to trial by an impartial jury because it is impossible in face of a flood tide of political pressures to grant a fair trial. If we are to break the grip of fear, it is necessary to change the procedures of investigation to conform to the spirit of our Bill of Rights. The Senatorial committee of investigation is one of the indispensable "checks and balances" of our government but it must protect individuals who are examined from losing their liberty and their property without due process of law. It is not within the concepts of our freedoms that appearance before a committee should involve a witness in unrelated political maneuvers nor should he be subject to unfair attacks made under Congressional immunity on the floor of either the House or Senate. No more cruel or unusual punishment can be devised than allowing a senator to make charges against individuals that he has not even attempted to substantiate with proof.

We have here a double problem to solve. One aspect of it concerns the security of the state, the other the security of the citizen. No one doubts that some appropriate method has to be devised to insure that people in key government positions are not subversive and are not serving as the agents of a foreign government. At the same time, where private citizens are concerned, we must realize that regardless of the existence of the cold war traditional American liberties are essential to the preservation of our constitutional system.

Of course we need in times like these an able and effective government agency to ascertain and check on persons who are subversive or foreign agents. The powers of this agency should be strictly limited and subject to constant review so that the agency does not gradually expand its function and bring under its jurisdiction people whose opinions are merely minority opinions.

The investigative committees of the Senate and House, with their broad powers, should of course be retained. Except for occasional aberrations such as those of the House Un-American Activities Committee under Congressmen Martin Dies and J. Parnell Thomas, these committees have only occasionally misused the investigative process. But committee procedures badly need re-examination when they deal with the sensitive areas of freedom and the rights of individuals. I am not qualified to make specific suggestions, but on the basis of my own experience it seems to me of crucial importance that an accuser should be compelled to confront the persons he accuses. It should be possible to work out some procedure for cross-examination by the accused and his counsel.

I am convinced by my experience that it is most important that the Senate and House should devise methods for restraining their own members. Within the Congress, there are long-established and elaborate rules to control the denunciation of members by members. There should also be rules to protect private citizens from denunciation on the floor of the Senate or House. Accusations against individuals should be made to the investigative agencies of the government, or in the way any other citizen has to make them — in public, where if they are libelous they may be tested in a court of law.

It has now become an urgent necessity to protect ourselves against abuse of the campaign for security by people who, while proclaiming their patriotism, may themselves be guided by motives that are sinister or selfish. Huey Long, a cynical and unprincipled politician, long ago warned us that if fascism ever came to America it would come disguised as one hundred per cent Americanism. By the same token, one hundred and fifty per cent denunciation of vaguely and imprecisely defined "Reds" may be a disguise for those who would destroy democracy.

In a democracy, the independent thinker is indispensable both to the planning of a successful foreign policy and to the maintenance of our democratic traditions. There is no way to maintain his independence and make it available to the service of the nation except by defending the freedom of inquiry and opinion of one and all. This does not mean that Communists who actually organize for subversive purposes should not feel the weight of the law, or fascists, or Ku Kluxers who organize to intimidate any section of our society, or lobbyists for any foreign power, whether or not they receive pay from a foreign source, if they resort to vilification and intimidation of their fellow citizens in the interests of a foreign power. But action for subversive purposes should be kept separate, in our minds as well as in our laws, from freedom of opinion. The freedom of the majority is only safe if the freedom of the minority — any minority — is protected.

While we are restoring to the individual the protections of the Fifth and Sixth Amendments, restoring the dignity of the Congress, restoring the confidence of the public, and thus breaking the grip of fear at home, we must also renew our attack on the problems that face us throughout the world. We must do so through open debate, strengthened by the conviction that all opinions, including minority opinions, are entitled to a full hearing. We must renew our faith in this traditional way of a democratic society. We must not allow ourselves to be bulldozed by those who in the name of "discipline" or a supposed "national emergency" try to insist that debate be suspended and that in face of a totalitarian menace we should adopt the most dangerous two-edged weapon of the enemy and make ourselves an authoritarian state.

As the heirs and guardians of the democratic tradition we must not allow men hungry for dictatorial power to impose upon us a regimented conformity of belief and opinion. But we must at the same time impose a reasoned and temperate self-discipline upon ourselves. Our right to resist dictatorship is rooted in our right to express opinions that are hateful to would-be dictators and authoritarians. The right to express an individual opinion is only secure if it includes the right to express a minority opinion; the right of minority opinion is only secure if it includes the right to express an unpopular opinion. Each of us must defend not only his own right to his own opinion. We must all unite to defend the right of any man to state opinions that challenge our own. What we must above all defend, as we value our own freedom, is the right of any man to his opinion, even if it offends powerful men or criticizes public authority.

We must defend this right because a healthy democratic society must be a living, growing, changing thing. To conserve its democratic character it must determine change, in the interest of the majority, through public debate which allows all minority interests and views to be represented and defended.

Those who demand that their own selfish interests be made paramount, and who for that reason oppose all change are obstructively antidemocratic. Those who seek first to encroach on and then to deny the rights and privileges of others in the greedy ambition to extend their own rights and privileges are active subverters of democracy.

It is more than our democratic right to oppose these men. It is the most sacred of our duties. Free men must stand together or fall one by one. The free man can only assert his freedom in association with other free men. Unless freedom is practiced, it withers. Therefore to write freedom into law is not enough. It must be affirmed and reaffirmed in every generation.